e-1/29/79

Fred C

Military strength in and around the Korean Peninsula

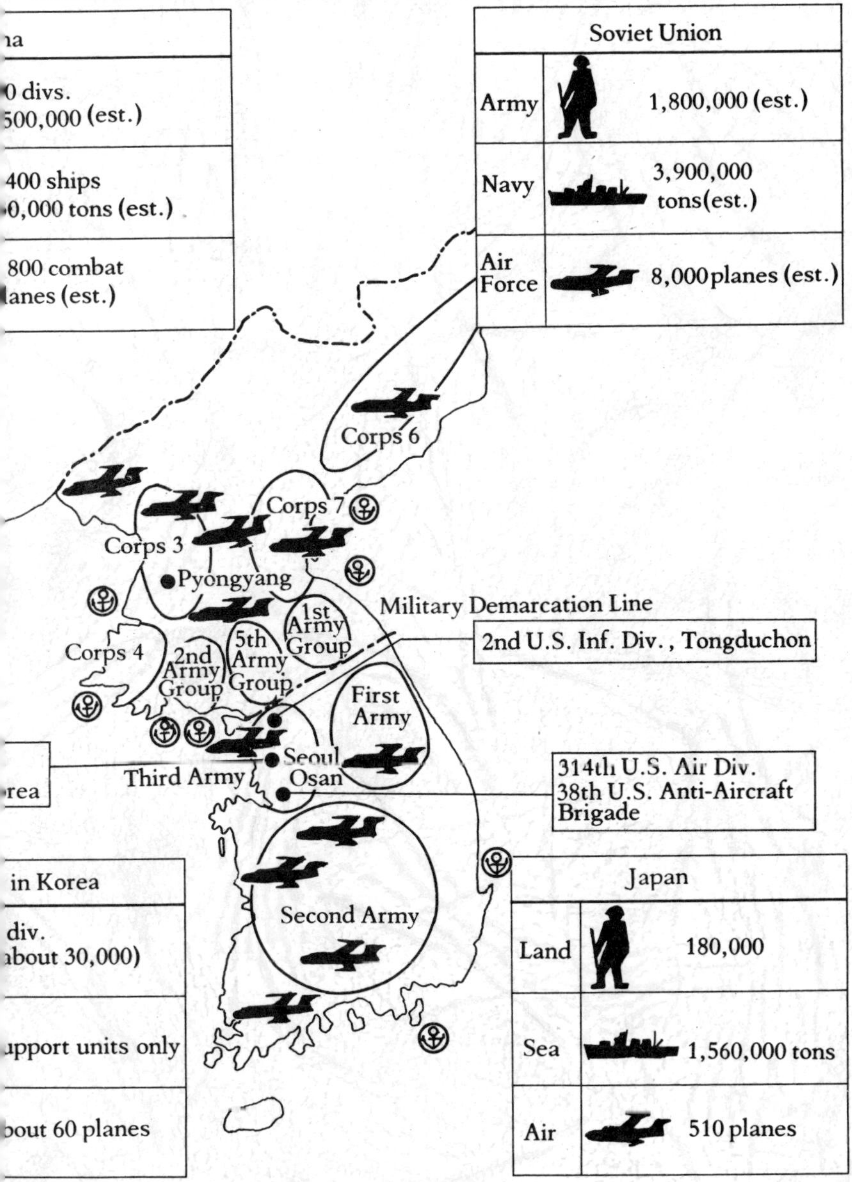

na
0 divs.
500,000 (est.)
400 ships
0,000 tons (est.)
800 combat
lanes (est.)
Soviet Union
Army
1,800,000 (est.)
Navy
3,900,000
tons(est.)
Air
Force
8,000planes (est.)
Corps 6
Corps 7
Corps 3
Pyongyang
Military Demarcation Line
1st
Army
Group
2nd U.S. Inf. Div., Tongduchon
Corps 4
2nd
Army
Group
5th
Army
Group
First
Army
Seoul
Osan
Third Army
rea
314th U.S. Air Div.
38th U.S. Anti-Aircraft
Brigade
in Korea
div.
about 30,000)
upport units only
bout 60 planes
Second Army
Japan
Land
180,000
Sea
1,560,000 tons
Air
510 planes

FUTURE
of
JAPAN
and the
KOREAN
PENINSULA

FUTURE
of
JAPAN
and the
KOREAN
PENINSULA

TSUNEARI FUKUDA

Translated from the Japanese by
K. JAHNG

HOLLYM INTERNATIONAL CORP.
Elizabeth, New Jersey   Seoul

FUTURE of JAPAN and the KOREAN PENINSULA
Copyright © 1978 by Hollym Corporation: Publishers

First English edition published in 1978
by Hollym International Corp.,
18 Donald Place, Elizabeth, New Jersey 07208 U.S.A.

Published simultaneously in Korea
by Hollym Corporation: Publishers
14-5 Kwan-chol Dong, Chong-no Ku, Seoul, Korea

ISBN: 0-930878-14-0
Library of Congress Catalog Card Number: 78-71337
Printed in Korea

This book is a translation of *Nihon no shorai—
Chosenhanto no subete*, which was published in Japan
by Takaki Shobo, Tokyo, © 1977 by Tsuneari Fukuda.

Publisher's Note

This book is a translation of Part I, *"Chosenhanto no kiki to nihon* (Crisis in the Korean Peninsula and Japan)" and Part II, *"Kitachosen to kankoku no hikaku* (North and South Korea Compared)" of *Nihon no shorai — Chosenhanto no subete* (Future of Japan—All About the Korean Peninsula) edited by Mr. Tsuneari Fukuda and published by Takaki Shobo, Tokyo, Japan, in 1977.

Part III, *"Chosenhanto no rekishi to bunka* (History and Culture of the Korean Peninsula)," has been omitted in the translation since this part deals with the historical Korean-Japanese relationship and is considered to be of less interest to English-speaking readers.

The observations of Professor Herbert Passin, one of the participants in Part I, have been edited by the professor.

Following the Oriental practice family names are given first for Orientals.

Unless specified otherwise and except for biographical data, the following books have been referred to in the preparation of most of the footnotes by the translator (excluding Nos. 3, 5, 10 and 11 that appear in the original Japanese edition): 1) Kungmin bangchop yon'guso (Institute for Research on Nation's Counter-Espionage), *Pukhan yongo taebaekwa*

(An Encyclopedia of North Korean Terminology), Seoul:
Kapcha Munwha-sa, 1976; 2) Nena Vreeland *et al.*, *Area
Handbook for North Korea*, Washington, D.C.: Government
Printing Office, 1976; 3) Yanaga Chitoshi, *Japan Since Perry*,
New York: Appleton-Century-Crofts, 1950.

The publisher is grateful to Mr. Tsuneari Fukuda and
to other participants for their cooperation and assistance in
the preparation of this book. He is also indebted to Professor
Fred M. Rosentreter (Chairman of the Department of History
at Southern Oregon College, and a visiting professor at
Dangook University in Seoul in 1977) and Mrs. Rosentreter,
Mr. Peter Finch (writer on Korean affairs, London) and
Mrs. Elizabeth Lee of Seoul for reading and refining the
draft translation.

The publisher is hopeful that this most candid and open-
hearted discussion by outstanding Japanese liberals and an
American professor will help the reader gain a new insight
into the future relations between Korea, Japan and the United
States.

July 1, 1978

Preface
to the original Japanese edition

The Japanese people tend to forget important things at important times. They seem unable even to perceive what is important. At the recent Japanese-Russian negotiations on fishing problems, Japan was annoyed by the Soviet Union's big-power chauvinism and her high-handedness. But Japan will not be taken seriously unless she means to be really angry. A diplomatic goal cannot be attained by sugar-coated eloquence or a treaty or communique alone. The Japanese do not perceive that simple logic. Nor are they aware why a diplomatic goal cannot be achieved that way. They censure the Soviet Union as an arrogant big-power but they forget how chauvinistic the Japanese were when Japan wooed China and broke off all of a sudden and without any mature deliberation her relations with the Nationalist Chinese Government. This was done in peace time when Nationalist China had done nothing hostile to Japan. If the Japanese are pretending not to be aware of that, they are downright selfish. They would better not to censure Russia's selfishness but to accept that the stronger will eventually prevail over the weaker.

The same holds true for her relations with South Korea. Japan finds fault with Seoul—the Kim Dae Jung Incident and others—as often as opportunity allows. On the other hand, the Japanese will not criticize the repressive regime in North Korea which cannot compare with the south in any respect. In the face of the withdrawal of the American combat ground troops from Korea—a situation that might develop into a conflagration which could engulf Japan—the Japanese look on with utter indifference. Perhaps they are not aware that a fire could start in the Korean Peninsula. Even if they do, they may think it is a fire burning inside the fireplace. They may not realize that it could spread like wildfire and threaten them at any moment.

However, it should be mentioned that soon after the discussion meeting—out of which this book emerged—the withdrawal plans became somewhat stalemated. But future prospects are by no means rosy since the United States' basic plan to pull out the troops remains unchanged.

Unlike South Korea, North Korea is extremely hard-pressed economically and may be tempted to invade the south even before all the American troops are phased out if she perceives the Americans are actually pulling out.

However, this does not mean that this discussion was intended to defend the south uncritically. This book is designed to bring to light what is virtually unknown to the readers of the Japanese press—the political and economic situations in the two halves of Korea—to correct the distorted information and criticisms on the two; and to explain why the security of Japan depends on the future turn of events in the Korean Peninsula.

What does the withdrawal of American troops from Korea mean, and what perils will it bring? These two questions were basic motives for writing this book. Before we discuss the important problem of the American troop withdrawal, we should see clearly how closely the developments in Korea are related to the future of the Japanese as a whole. A more important problem for the Japanese is that they do not consider such important matters sufficiently.

Whether they are living in the south or the north, the people residing in the Korean Peninsula and the Korean residents in Japan were subject to Japan's colonial rule for about 40 years until the end of World War II. Japan and the Japanese benefitted from this occupation in one way or another. Conversely, the Korean people and the Korean residents in Japan suffered many hardships because of Japan's colonial rule. Many of them fought and died as Japanese soldiers or were otherwise lost in action, leaving behind them not a few bereaved families. I do not mean that we have to atone for our guilt. A fact is a fact and one cannot pretend not to be aware of this. Some argue that Japan gave up Korea when the San Francisco Treaty was signed after the war; the Korean Peninsula is not Japan's business now; and we should not care what happens there. These people may think it is   irritating that the United States imposed the "Korea clause" on Japan. They forget the past. They ignore the fact that South Korea belongs to the free world and is a friend of Japan. And these Japanese tend to criticize South Korea as if they were outsiders.

The year before last I attended a symposium that was sponsored by the South Korean Academy of Arts and had an opportunity to visit Kyongju, the erstwhile capital of the Silla dynasty (B.C.57 - A.D.935), and Puyo and Kongju, the ancient capitals of the Paekche dynasty (B.C.18 - A.D.600). I also visited places of interest in Seoul and caught a glimpse of the Yi dynasty (1392 - 1910) cultural heritage.

In urban as well as rural communities, the whole country is vibrant with life and energy and a zeal to build the nation. Except for a few anti-establishment figures, the Korean people are enjoying fully—as their Japanese counterparts are—the rights to spend as consumers and travel as they like. I saw for myself that the country is reaching the level of the advanced countries. South Korea is not a somber country; she is bright and full of life. Grafters and double-crossers exist in South Korea just as they do in the United States, Japan and other countries of the free world. I met Korean opposition leaders and anti-establishment activists. I also met Mr. Kim Dae Jung and listened to him as he set forth his views for several hours. However, they all failed to convince me. After the trip to Korea, I received a greeting card from Mr. Lee Chul Seung who newly had taken over the reins of the New Democratic Party—the opposition party. From the card it was clear that the oppositionists in South Korea are not simply obsessed with obstructing the government, that in principle they give solid support to government policy, and that they are coping seriously with the urgent task of contributing to national security and modernization of their country.

The participants in the discussion meeting were not biased against North Korea. We tried only to weigh facts and correlate them to each other and to see whether North Korea—be she a friend or enemy of ours—can sit with us at the same table or can be treated in the way we treat other countries. I stress again that to us Japanese the problem of the Korean Peninsula is important, perhaps more important today than it was under Japanese rule (1910 - 1945). Once the Japanese meddled in Korea's affairs too officiously, and now they are doing just the reverse of that—showing total indifference to the developments in the peninsula. We should not be allowed to commit such follies again. In order not to do so, we should first understand the history of Japanese-Korean relations—relations characterized by ambivalence—from the standpoint not only of the Japanese but of the Koreans. We should then proceed to seek ways and means whereby we can make up for past mistakes and look forward to a constructive future relationship.

As for the title of this book an explanation is in order. As is evident in Part III, the face of the country—which the Korean people have built—has changed many times. In the

postwar period, the area north of the 38th Parallel came under
the rule of the Democratic People's Republic of Korea
while that south of the Parallel is governed by the Republic
of Korea. Therefore, we can think of no appropriate general
term. The title "Korean Peninsula" represents only a geo-
graphic entity. In this book the peninsula is referred to by
different designations, as occasion demands.

September 13, 1977   TSUNEARI FUKUDA

Contents

Publisher's Note   v
Preface to the original Japanese edition   vii

PART I   CRISIS IN THE KOREAN PENINSULA AND JAPAN
Profiles of the Participants   5

THE AMERICAN MILITARY PRESENCE DETERS WAR   7

Nothing is more foolish than withdrawal   7
Human rights diplomacy hard to understand   14
President Carter acts arbitrarily   18
Japan takes no action   21
Strange mentality of the Japanese press   25
The curious position of Professor Reischauer   30
Love-hate relationship between Japan and America   34
Is America trustworthy?   39

U.S. SLIGHTS ASIA   45

Uncertainty of the American commitment to defend Japan   45
The air force can withdraw at any time   52
"No threat from the north," a downright lie   56
War ruins everything   61
Five western islands in a touch-and-go situation   64
What if South Korea is communized?   67
America's current irresponsibility   70

WHAT CAN BE DONE ABOUT MUTUAL DIS-
TRUST BETWEEN JAPAN, KOREA AND AMER-
ICA?   73

Japanese lack common sense in international affairs   73
North Korea's mobilization capability is the greatest
    in the world   76
It's Japan's problem after all   80
Japan overestimated   85
What America wants Japan to do   89

PART II SOUTH AND NORTH KOREA COMPARED
Profiles of the Participants   99

POLITICS, THE ECONOMY, AND ORDINARY LIFE
IN NORTH KOREA   101

How North Korean statistics are to be read   101
A difference between a market economy and a com-
    mand economy   106
The difference between southern and northern
    national goals   112
A free society cannot be built in a day   114
Gen. Kim Il Sung returns home by Russian tank   120
Facts about Kim Il Sung-ism, the one and only guid-
    ing ideology   127
North Korea is a Kim's dynasty   133
Peculiar social structure and a "back-number" system   136
Foreign relations completely deadlocked   142
Food shortage worsening   145
People depend on blackmarketeering for a living   149
Indoctrination halts production   152

POLITICS, THE ECONOMY, AND ORDINARY LIFE
IN SOUTH KOREA   158

The Park Chung Hee Government and prosperity
    in the 1970's   158
Kim Dae Jung does not represent the masses   163
Democratic *Saemaul* (New Community) Movement   166

South Korea is not a dictatorship   170
People are watching closely   175
"White Capitalism" belittles Asia   179
Economic aid is one thing, "connection" another   185
Yardstick for measuring freedom   188
Koreans are not a whining people   191

APPENDICES

1. Chart of government structure of the south   197
2. Chart of government structure of the north   198
3. Defense and military organizational chart of the north   199
4. Geneaology of Kim Il Sung   200
5. Major industries in North Korea   201
6. Economic comparison of the south and the north   202

FUTURE
of
JAPAN
and the
KOREAN
PENINSULA

PART I

CRISIS
in the
KOREAN PENINSULA
and
JAPAN

Participants :

KASE HIDEAKI

HERBERT PASSIN

MURAMATSU TAKESHI

WAKAMATSU JUGO

FUKUDA TSUNEARI

From left: Messrs. Wakamatsu, Passin, Kase, Muramatsu, Fukuda

Profiles of the Participants

Mr. Kase Hideaki

Born in 1936; studied at Keio, Yale, and Columbia Univs.; editor of TBS Britannica; adviser to Hudson Institute and commentator on foreign affairs.

Prof. Herbert Passin

Born in 1916; promoter of the Japanese-American Assembly (the Shimoda Conference); Chairman, Dept. of Sociology, Columbia University.

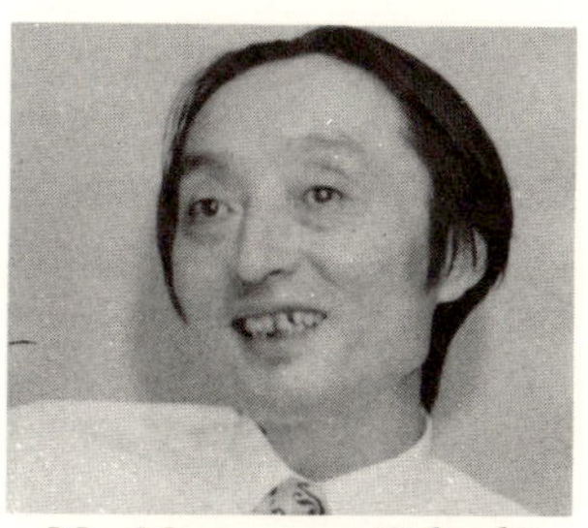

Mr. Muramatsu Takeshi

Born in 1929; B.A. in French literature, Tokyo Univ.; taught at Rikkyo and Kyoto Industrial Univs.; commentator on political, social and literal affairs; professor at Tsukuba Univ.

Mr. Wakamatsu Jugo

Born in Manchuria in 1921; studied at Takushoku Univ.; reserve naval fight officer (1st Lt.); commentator on Chinese and military affairs.

Mr. Fukuda Tsuneari

Born in 1912; B.A. in English, Tokyo Univ., 1936; commentator, playwright; Chairman, Modern Playwrights Association and professor at Kyoto Industrial Univ.

The American military presence deters war

Nothing is more foolish than withdrawal

Kase: The Korean Peninsula is not only closest to Japan but has an important strategic value. Here the interests of the four major powers—the Soviet Union, China, Japan and the United States—clash head-on. Along the 38th Parallel troops of the Republic of Korea (South) and the Democratic People's Republic of Korea (North) confront each other. Nowhere in the world are such a large number of troops concentrated in confrontation as in the narrow Korean Peninsula. The withdrawal of the American troops in Korea was originally planned during the Nixon Administration. By March 1971, 20,000 American troops, one-third of the total strength of the American military presence in Korea, had been pulled out. One of the two American infantry divisions stationed midway between the armistice line and Seoul, the 7th Infantry Division, is already gone. And the remaining 2nd Infantry Division is to be phased out, too.

During the recent U.S. election campaign, presidential candidate Jimmy Carter promised to make "full consultations" with Japan and Korea over the withdrawal of the American troops from Korea. Despite this promise, he, on assuming the presidency, made just such a one-sided decision without the promised "full consultations" with the two countries, and has forced his decision upon them.

On January 20, President Carter moved to the White House and around the end of the month, sent Vice President Walter Mondale to Japan to notify her of the decision to withdraw American troops from Korea over a five-year period. Later in July, when Defense Secretary Harold Brown visited Seoul, the schedule of withdrawal was made public. From this announcement we see that President Carter's original plan has been somewhat modified due in part to resistance from the Pentagon: 6,000 troops will be withdrawn initially, followed by the gradual phase-out of the remainder. The headquarters of the 2nd Infantry Division and two brigades will remain until the final phase of the withdrawal. However, the basic plan of withdrawing the troops over a period of five years remains unchanged. I think that the strategic location South Korea occupies in the free world is very important. Thus it is hard for most of us Japanese—not only the government officials concerned but the general public—to understand why the U.S. made such a decision in such a hasty way.

Let's start our discussion from this point. The hasty U.S. decision may create distrust between Japan and the U.S. Mr. Passin, would you begin with your comment on this point?

Passin: Let me say first that I am in a somewhat awkward position. I do not want to be put in the position of having to defend President Carter's views, since I happen to disagree with them rather extensively.

But if I were called upon to explain the reasons for the decision to withdraw American troops from Korea, I would list two principal ones. One is the post-Vietnam trauma. Many feel that America is overinvolved in Asia and therefore should disengage herself from the area. There is a widely prevalent fear among Americans that we made a grave mistake in Vietnam and that we may be repeating the same mistake in Korea.

Another is Mr. Carter's feeling that he should honor his campaign pledge. I think he is motivated by these two factors.

Kase: What caused him to make such a commitment?

Passin: It probably started out as a political strategem and he fell into a trap of his own making. (*Laughter*.) That is, in order to be elected, he needed to appeal to the old McGovern people, the leftwing of the Democratic Party. So he came up with the plan to withdraw the troops, which was the kind of thing that would appeal to them.

Muramatsu: In his famous "again speech," Franklin Roosevelt said: "I have said before, but I shall say it again and again and again: Your boys are not going to be sent into any foreign wars." In fact, however, he had already decided on participation and had promised Winston Churchill to enter World War II.

Lyndon B. Johnson also said during his election campaign that he would not get involved in the Vietnam war. But after he was President he did get involved in the war. American Presidents, therefore, have not always done what they pledged during their election campaign, but have even acted in contrary fashion.

This is tolerated in the world of politics. Circumstances change. There will be no contending against that.

Then what matters is not campaign pledges, but why a politician feels he has to take such foolish action after he has assumed the position of responsibility.

Passin: I would suggest that there are two factors involved here. First, not all American presidents are Franklin Roosevelts or Lyndon Johnsons. Each have different characters, and it is mistaken to assume that all American presidents act the same way.

Secondly, the Korean decision came on the heels of Watergate. The American people had become very suspicious of presidential promises. President Carter may have concluded that it was the better part of valor to keep this promise.

Muramatsu: Mr. Carter said that if Soviet Russia invaded Yugoslavia after Tito's death, the U.S. would not come to her aid. Will he keep this pledge, too? This is an important question.

Passin: I regret to say that as of now he would probably keep his word and not come to her aid. This will of course depend upon the future turn of events, and the problem isn't an easy one. But I think that it is unlikely that the U.S. would come to her aid at anytime in the foreseeable future.

Kase: But, to begin with, President Carter cannot keep all his commitments including those regarding economic policies. Ever since the election campaign, Mr. Carter has said that North Korea will not invade the south even if the American troops in Korea are withdrawn. He continues that since the South Korean armed forces are to be modernized over the next 5 years, the south can defend herself in case North Korea invades her. If South Korea comes under North Korean attack, he adds, the U.S. will support her. But he doesn't say that if the north swoops down on the south after the withdrawal of the American ground forces, he will commit U.S. ground troops to the defense of Korea. Maybe, only American naval and air forces will be committed. Well, the U.S. military leaders aren't too happy about withdrawing the American ground forces in Korea.

Now, let me ask Mr. Wakamatsu whether it is correct to assume that the withdrawal of the American ground troops over a five-year period will not threaten South Korea. From the point of view of a military expert, please.

Wakamatsu: The threat from the north may decrease a little when the South Korean armed forces have been greatly strengthened in the five-year period, but the absence of the American ground troops will be a decisive weakness. Also, it should be noted that the Forces Improvement Plan currently under way in the south is said to have been set in motion only last year. Unless it is carried out effectively, the gap currently existing between the military strength of the south and that of the north won't be filled.

Here a survey of the military forces of both sides is in order. The south has a 520,000-man army, 18 infantry divisions, 7 reserve divisions for training recruits and for rear defenses, 2 armored brigades, 5 airborne brigades, and a 20,000-man marine division—though this isn't under the command of army. The marines are said to be the finest land combat unit. Tanks total about 900, armored vehicles 500 and fieldpieces 2,000. The navy has about 100 ships and the air force is comprised of about 200 planes including 50 F86's, 70 F5's, and 70 F4's.

Against this, the North Koreans have a 440,000-man army, 23 infantry divisions, 2 armored divisions, 4 infantry brigades, a light infantry brigade, 8 brigades of special warfare units—mostly for guerrilla warfare, and 5 armored regiments. They have about 2,000 tanks, 750 armored vehicles, 3,000 fieldpieces, 5,500 anti-aircraft guns, and 24 Russian FROG missiles with a range of about 70 Km, a range easily making Seoul vulnerable from the northern side of the Military Demarcation Line. The navy has 450 ships including over 10 submarines. It also has about 20 small missile boats carrying Styx ship-to-ship missiles. The air force has 650 planes including 550 MIG-17, -19, -21, SU-7 fighters and other fighter-bombers. Besides, it has about 100 IL-28 bombers. To this I must add paramilitary units such as the Worker-Peasant Red Guards,[1] the Young Red Guards[2] and others. These are powerful units that can be thrown instantly into land warfare.

Thus, in terms of the tanks that provide a nucleus for land warfare, the north has twice as many as the south: as for the air force, an indispensable element in a modern war, the north has roughly three times as many planes as the south—though the planes have different performances and purposes allowing no hasty judgment on their superiority and inferiority. The American forces in Korea make up for these weaknesses both in quality and quantity.

Also the deployment of the American troops in Korea has an important meaning. The U.S. 2nd Infantry Division is deployed to the northeast of Seoul, the invasion route along which the North Korean troops spearheaded by tanks made their inroad into Seoul from Chorwon during the Korean War. Such deployment of American troops means that when North Korea makes another attempt at invading the south, her troops will unavoidably have to engage American troops. If and when North Korea decides to attack Seoul, she must be ready for an encounter with the American troops—and for the United States as an enemy. Since North Korea doesn't like an idea of fighting the U.S. directly, the presence of the U.S. troops in this area provides a mighty deterrent to the outbreak of a war on the peninsula. I don't know when, but I'm sure that when they cease to be stationed there, a perilous situation will develop.

1. Estimated at 128,000 as of October 1975, and comprising all able-bodied men from 18 to 45 and single women in the ages of 18 to 30, the Red Guard is an auxiliary military force. The training is conducted one to two hours daily or 500 hours a year.

2. Mostly composed of students, the Young Red Guard is a vigilante-type militia under the control of the party for protection of Kim Il Sung and Pyong-yang city in time of emergency. Its number was estimated at 700,000 in the early 1970's.

Also it's well-nigh impossible to fill in completely the great military gaps between the north and the south—as I have already suggested—over a four- to five-year period. While the south is beefing up her armed forces, we cannot imagine that the north will stand by idly.

Kase: When we look at the military balance between the south and the north, our first concern is how Soviet Russia may act. For example, during the last Arab-Israeli war Soviet Russia supplied a huge number of tanks to the Arab states and to Egypt in a very brief span of time. Since North Korea borders on Soviet Russia, the latter will certainly supply a large quantity of weaponry to the former in a short period of time when a war breaks out. This will further tip the present military balance in favor of the north.

Another uncertainty. Carter says in case of war the south is capable of defending herself independently. As we do not wish to see a war break out, we are primarily concerned about how this can be prevented. Thus we value highly the presence of American troops in Korea as a deterrent to war. If a war comes and even if the south has successfully held back the initial attack, we Japanese will get into trouble, to say nothing of the Koreans themselves, who will have to experience another tragedy.

Wakamatsu: You're right. I think the presence of the American ground troops itself has great merit. Mr. Carter says, "It's O.K. as we will support the south with our naval and air forces even if the ground troops are withdrawn." Only a real war will prove whether it's O.K. or not. The withdrawal of the ground troops will inevitably remove the deterrent to war. The central problem is not how to win a war or to drive back a North Korean attack, but how to prevent war itself. I think this is the crucial problem. I believe the naval and air forces—however greatly they may be strengthened—will not be able to play completely the role of the ground troops.

Human rights diplomacy hard to understand

Fukuda: Another problem is President Carter's human rights diplomacy. In a five-year's time, the south will be on a par with the north in fighting strength, or hopefully it will surpass the north. This is what President Carter thinks.

If Mr. Carter's perception is correct, the Park Chung Hee Government will have to develop more stringent policies to regulate more severely the people's daily life as consumers and to restrict freedoms—though human rights there are already posing a problem. Then, what on earth is President Carter's human rights diplomacy supposed to do? Is it a pretence or does he really mean it? I am most curious to know.

Carter may convince us if he says, as has Mr. Passin, that America is fed up with Vietnam, that her hands are full taking care of her own interests and that she has ceased being a world policeman. But human rights diplomacy is different. If it is applied blindly, the south will be driven to take harsher repressive measures. Human rights diplomacy is certainly meant for the Soviets, but America should be more prudent in dealing with the human rights issue in South Korea, a member of the free world. I seriously wonder whether Mr. Carter is conducting the affairs of the state as a politician and a realist or as a fundamentalist having an absolute belief in the infallibility of the Scriptures. I can't fathom whether Mr. Carter is speaking as a Christian or as a down-to-earth realist who believes that everything will be all right only if the U.S. is all right, much as I find it hard to know if the Japanese Socialist Party really intends to take power or thinks it safer to stay away from power. (*Laughter*.)

Muramatsu: Let me add a little to what Mr. Fukuda has said. Neither can I understand. There are two things that the Carter Administration is doing that I don't understand at all.

One is Mr. Carter's excessively emotional actions. He abruptly recalled a Chief of Staff of the American troops in Korea, a man who had done nothing particularly wrong in terms of violation of orders. Since the American troops in Korea are under the command of the Pacific Forces, it would have been reasonable for the Commander-in-Chief of the Pacific Forces to have given him a reprimand or some such inasmuch as this wasn't a case of gross insubordination. However, Mr. Carter, a President of a country, grappled earnestly with a Chief of Staff of an American corps abroad simply because the general's critical statement was published in the *Washington Post*. Having recalled the general, Mr. Carter may have found himself in an awkward position. Late in May he reassigned him to the important post of Chief of Staff of a U.S. Army corps at home (U.S. Army Forces Command at Fort Mcpherson in Georgia). Such being the case, it would have been far better not to have recalled the general at all.

Mr. Carter declared that he would not hesitate to use nuclear weapons should the North Koreans invade southward. But on another occasion he said that U.S. tactical nuclear weapons would be withdrawn from Korea. I wonder how he can reconcile these two positions. It is obvious even to a layman how difficult it would be to send back for redeployment tactical nuclear weapons once withdrawn. There isn't any consistency between what Mr. Carter says and what he does. This is the first thing that I do not understand about Mr. Carter.

My second point may overlap with what Mr. Fukuda has said. Mr. Carter advocates human rights diplomacy. It may be said that human rights diplomacy has existed in the U.S. ever since President Woodrow Wilson. The concept of human rights is very vague, but the right to live lies at the heart of it. To the South Koreans, the first and foremost question is how to survive. But let us set aside this question for now. Since it was Franklin Roosevelt who advocated the Four Freedoms, it can be said that human rights diplomacy is but an extension of the Wilsonian and Roosevelt's diplomacy. Now the problem is that if one country forces her moral values upon others, this will be followed by intervention in internal affairs. This is bound to incur public censure. Thus moral diplomacy inevitably leads to a policy of intervention, a policy embodying excessive responsibilities.

As Wilson intervened in World War I, Roosevelt intervened in World War II. John Kennedy may in a sense rank among them. During the Kennedy era, the number of American military advisers in Vietnam jumped from 600 to 13,000. Therefore, if a country adopts a human rights policy, she must be ready to accept the responsibility commensurate with it.

Historically, America has another tradition, one of realistic diplomacy as followed by Theodore Roosevelt, Richard M. Nixon and Henry A. Kissinger. It is comparatively isolationist in nature and doesn't force morals upon other countries. Instead, it seeks a realistic position to keep the U.S. free from any external intervention. This in itself has a justifiable rationale.

Now, President Carter preaches human rights diplomacy on the one hand while he tends to apply an isolationist policy in Asia on the other. He combines two diametrically opposed concepts into one policy. It is natural and reasonable for us to be skeptical whether the President is seriously considering implementing such essentially contradictory policies. Never in the history of the United States have isolationism and morality —as represented by human rights diplomacy—been compatible. I think it's the first time in the history of American foreign policy that they are applied indiscriminately.

Fukuda: To return to the first point posed by Mr. Muramatsu, Maj. Gen. John Singlaub, formerly the third-ranking officer in Korea, was removed on impulse. In short, this was an act of despotism. The Japanese press lauded the removal as an example of civilian control, but the action really was despotic.

Muramatsu: It was the way a feudal lord acted.

Fukuda: Then they can't characterize President Park Chung Hee's way of ruling as despotic. So many contradictions! And I wonder if President Carter is acting in his right mind, or if he is a realist who uses the human rights issue as a tool of diplomacy. He hasn't applied the human rights diplomacy to South Korea yet, but I fear he may do so as an excuse for withdrawal of the American troops.

Passin: I, too, have some doubts about President Carter's human rights diplomacy. But we can't limit the human rights issue to the question of diplomacy. Human rights are an issue whether they become involved with foreign policy or not. The problem is to what extent, and when and where these two stand in what relationship to one another.

Take Hitler's Germany for example: We should have taken a stand right from the start against the persecution of the Jews. Unfortunately, however, we did not, nor did any other so-called civilized country. The result was that 6 million Jews were slaughtered and much of the world was driven to war.

If we could simply turn our backs on the violation of human rights anywhere in the world, there would be no problem. In the past, it was easier to be indifferent because usually people did not know what was happening. But, today we cannot. Thanks to the tremendous advancement in modern communications, people can watch TV in their living rooms and see what is happening even in remote corners of the world. It is no longer possible for us to close our eyes and ears to this steady inflow of information from abroad.

One of the major reasons that the general public in the United States reacted so strongly to the Vietnam war was that they sat around the supper table at night watching on the evening news scenes of killings that had taken place that very day—12,000 miles away. These experiences were used by opponents of the war to intensify public opposition. Now, the same technology keeps people aware of violations of human rights all over the world, particularly in Communist countries and in some of the developing countries. Therefore many people feel that President Carter's human rights diplomacy is not being carried out vigorously enough. The problem is not simple; it is, on the contrary, very complex.

Fukuda: But it is certain that South Korea is a free country where no such infringement of human rights exists as to make it a target of human rights diplomacy. The country should not be confused with Nazi Germany, Soviet Russia, China, or North Korea.

President Carter acts arbitrarily

Kase: Certainly, the Japanese have no right to intervene in the human rights matter in other countries. It would be illogical for us to do so. To hark back to the subject of Major Gen. Singlaub, the *Washington Post* printed what the general said apparently off the record.

Muramatsu: His case was quite different from the dismissal of Gen. Douglas MacArthur. MacArthur was already the Chief of Staff of the U.S. Army during World War I and his later aides included Dwight D. Eisenhower as a major. MacArthur was an elder in the military, leading all other generals on the seniority list. At the time he was the Army Chief of Staff, Harry S. Truman was a timber dealer or something like that. Some critics have even likened Truman to an insurance salesman beside MacArthur.

Moreover, MacArthur defied the President's order, and Truman had to wield his powers as President. We can understand why Truman had had to take the position he did, laying aside the question of whether he was right or not. Even if we take into consideration Truman's emotional predisposition, we are somewhat sympathetic with his position. But Carter's way is completely different. I think it is strange indeed that a country like the U.S., valuing as it does law and order, should tolerate Carter's arbitrary way of doing things.

Kase: There is another difference between the cases of MacArthur and Singlaub. When MacArthur proposed to bomb Manchuria, his opinion represented the minority in the military and the Pentagon.

Most of the military leaders sided with Truman and preferred to act with prudence. As regards the question of withdrawal of the U.S. ground troops from Korea, the Pentagon and the military—I met some Joint Chiefs of Staff personnel —all opposed it. The problem is that Carter is forcing the plan over this opposition.

Wakamatsu: The Pentagon let it be known later that it had not been consulted on the withdrawal of the ground troops in Korea. Therefore, the complaint and resistance of the military against what it considers an unrealistic policy are natural.

Passin: So many issues have been raised here! (*Laughter.*) The first is the motive for President Carter's diplomacy. Mr. Fukuda said Carter is acting as a fundamentalist Christian, but I don't think that is what is involved in this case. I have no way of knowing, of course, what he is thinking, but I feel quite sure he is not acting out of any simple religious motive.

At the time Mr. Carter became president, he was virtually unknown to the American people and therefore did not have their unqualified confidence. As a consequence, he was undoubtedly somewhat unsure of himself. He was a local politician, not a member of the Washington Establishment, and he may therefore have felt that he had to put forward some policies that were sure to convince all those who were watching his every move.

I would imagine that he calculated that in the Democratic Party, he was least trusted by the leftwing of the party; he did not have to worry about the rightwing and the middle-of-the-road. His strategy, therefore, may very well have been to set forward some policies designed to appeal to the leftwing Democrats. Obviously when a president commits himself publicly to a policy, there is a good chance that he might become its prisoner. I would suppose that when he announced it during the campaign he did not seriously think about the consequences.

The Singlaub case may be interpreted as a military challenge to a civilian president. President Carter may therefore have felt it necessary to do something to show that he was a strong president. It is significant, however, that he did not discharge General Singlaub but reassigned him.

Regarding the next and the fundamental question, I am not sure why or from what motives he adopted his Korean position. But I can think of two possibilities.

First, if you take the position it is not the responsibility of the United States to defend Korea, then troops there must be withdrawn. There are many Americans who hold this point of view. But, this is not, I think, President Carter's position. What, then, is the reason? First, the quality and quantity of the ground troops should be taken into consideration. This .is a practical question. Is a full division of ground troops necessary in Korea? May it not be possible to halve the number without endangering Korean defense, since it is equipped with highly sophisticated weapons? Even some Americans who favor the U.S. defense of South Korea take this position.

For others, the primary consideration is the budgetary savings that could be made by withdrawing American ground troops. This type of argument is understandable. Not being an expert in this field, I cannot judge it, but I understand this kind of reasoning in principle. However, I don't understand why President Carter is being so vague about it and why he is causing our allies so much anxiety.

Another thing that worries me is that while the United States has been talking about withdrawal—and it has been for a long time—it has not seen fit to strengthen the South Korean air force, nor has it gone about the modernization of Korea's armed forces as vigorously as might have been expected. I think this is strange.

Kase: The Five-Year Modernization Plan of the South Korean armed forces begun in the 1970's has not progressed at all. Today it is still referred to as a plan and its implementation is being put off.

Japan takes no action

Passin: There is another rather curious problem here that is not obvious to everyone. The president and his associates, I would think, have serious doubts as to whether Japan would allow the United States to use its bases in Japan should there be trouble on the Korean Peninsula.

Kase: You mean an advance consultation between Japan and the U.S. on the use of the American bases in Japan for making sorties into Korea—whether the Japanese Government will permit it or not?

Passin: Americans are increasingly doubtful on that point. Many Japanese tell their American friends, publicly and privately, that the defense of South Korea is indispensable to the security of Japan. But, when they are asked what Japan is going to do about it, the answer is invariably "we can't do anything." If the matter is so important to the Japanese, why don't they do something about it?

Many Japanese ask their American friends to do whatever is necessary to defend South Korea. But these very

Japanese who expect the United States to bear the burden will lean back and do nothing when the question of using the U.S. military bases in Japan comes up.

At the very minimum, we should be able to count on Japan's cooperation if we are expected to take military action and make the sacrifices for the defense of Korea that we are assured by the Japanese are vital for Japan's own defense. This means that we have to be sure that we can use the U.S. military facilities in Japan.

The situation is paradoxical and ambiguous, and one result is that many Americans, both government officials and private citizens, have come to doubt Japan's sincerity. If South Korea is essential to Japan, Japan should be willing to contribute to its defense. Japan should support South Korea militarily, or if that is not possible, at least, support the U.S. effort. Some Americans now feel that Japan should be made to confront this issue squarely.

Fukuda: That's the point! In my book, *Nichibei ryo kokumin ni utsutaeru* (An Appeal to Japanese and American Peoples), I stressed this point. I have so far found fault, rather deliberately, with President Carter and America since I wanted to evoke the kind of response that Mr. Passin gave just now. (*Laughter.*) Certainly, Japan isn't entitled to take exception to the withdrawal of the American ground troops in Korea. We the minority oppose the withdrawal and the majority of Japanese remain apathetic. Who is responsible for the latter attitude? The Americans. So I want to appeal to the peoples of the two countries.

Why is Mr. Carter saying so ridiculous a thing that America defends South Korea not for the sake of South Korea, but for that of Japan? For one thing, this ignores the human rights of the Korean people. For another, America is willing to defend a Japan that is unwilling to defend herself. It may be silly to say now, but South Korea is far more determined to defend herself.

Kase: Now, let me raise some fundamental questions. When North Vietnam launched a large scale offensive in 1975, the United States Congress turned down President Ford's request for provision of emergency aid to South Vietnam. Had the United States provided emergency assistance to South Vietnam then, that country might have not crumbled in the way she did. South Vietnam was denied assistance and fell. And the United States demonstrated by deed that she would no longer defend the Asian continent.

Another thing is that before the collapse of Vietnam, the White House and the Department of State made a point of telling the Congress and the public, when explaining the rationale of the American military presence in South Korea, that it was necessary to defend South Korea. But since the fall of Vietnam they have changed their position, stating that their presence in Korea is necessary for the defense of Japan.

Also I don't understand why during the presidential campaign Mr. Carter did not mention the human rights issue at all when he proposed the phase-out of the American forces. At that time, he appealed to the American voters on the basis of cutting the military budget.

When we ask the Pentagon whether the withdrawal can actually reduce the military budget, they say it is more economical to station an American infantry division in Korea than in the United States proper. Further, it is reported that all the equipment of the U.S. troops will be transferred to the South Korean armed forces when withdrawal takes place, but it will cost some 500 million dollars to procure the equipment anew for the division.

Recently, I was shocked to learn that the 2nd Infantry Division now in Korea is not going to be pulled out for defense of the United States, but be stationed on the East Coast as a reserve force for possible deployment in Europe. Now the explanation of saving money becomes nonsense.

Passin: President Carter did mention a cut in the military budget during the election. And it is also true that some advocates of withdrawal have based their argument on this. But no one in a responsible position in the Administration has ever publicly cited this as a reason. Someone must have made a rough estimate of the money the troop withdrawal would save. But the amounts were apparently so small that no one official has mentioned it.

Being ignorant of this, many Americans think that the withdrawal policy is part of the campaign promise to slash the defense budget.

Kase: To return to the withdrawal of the American ground troops in Korea, something must be done before the withdrawal.

First, North Korea should recognize the right of South Korea to survive.

Second is the so-called cross recognition: China and Soviet Russia recognize South Korea in return for recognition of North Korea by Japan and the United States. It would be quite abnormal for the American troops in Korea to furl their banners and go home before these conditions have been fulfilled.

Fukuda: For the United States it would be easier to push the cross recognition matter while she still has her troops in Korea. After all her troops have been withdrawn, she won't have a bargaining chip left vis-a-vis North Korea.

Muramatsu: Legally, the withdrawal will engender problems. And in terms of cost-effectiveness analysis, it would be far more economical if America would preserve the stability in Asia by keeping an army division in Korea.

The American troops in Europe comprise eleven divisions including the marines and two independent brigades deployed in the southern part of West Germany. Besides, there are 7,000 tactical nuclear weapons in Europe. Compared with this,

American military presence in Korea is far more economical.

Kase: The Carter Administration seems to be considering providing South Korea with additional assistance of 1,900 million dollars—500 million dollars worth of military equipment that the American troops will turn over to South Korea at the time of their withdrawal and another 1,400 million dollars in Foreign Military Sales Credits subject to congressional approval. It's possible that the withdrawal will be carried out without the Congress having approved the appropriation.

Strange mentality of the Japanese press

Kase: When Mr. Passin spoke, I felt that to the Americans Vietnam and South Korea are not distinguishable.

Vietnam and South Korea are quite different politically and economically. South Korea is very stabilized as we shall see when we go there. At no time in the history of Korea has the living of the masses been more secure. Some criticisms are being levelled at the present government, but the welfare of the Koreans has never been better.

Passin: I didn't say that there wasn't a difference. But you may be right, however, most Americans don't recognise the difference.

Kase: Much to my annoyance, even American intellectuals do not distinguish between Vietnam and Korea.

Passin: Yes, in general, you are right. That the general public cannot distinguish South Korea from Vietnam can be interpreted in the following way: When the U.S. intervened in Vietnam, there was a national consensus. Here was a poor little Asian country being attacked by the north and valiantly fighting to defend its independence. Few Americans had any doubts that the U.S. should give a helping hand. But these ideas, which had been taken for granted, suddenly turned sour. People no longer believe in them. The U.S. has under-gone such a traumatic experience that people have come to think that the ideas themselves are wrong.

Now, the arguments for stationing U.S. troops in Korea sound very similar to those justifying our Vietnam involve-ment. Many Americans began to feel that since we were wrong in Vietnam, perhaps we are wrong in Korea too and that our Korea policy should now be reexamined.

Another reason for this change is a finicky American sense of morality that holds that we should only support democracies. At first, Americans thought South Vietnam was democratic, but as the war progressed they gradually came to change their mind. Some people have come to have the same feeling about South Korea. We should not help non-democratic countries, whether they are communist or not. Therefore, as long as South Korea is under dictatorial rule, it is no different from the north, and we have no particular responsibility for its defense. Many American Congressmen feel this way.

In spring last year, I presented testimony at a hearing of the Foreign Relations Committee of the Congress and was surprised to learn there were so many people in the Congress who thought this way.

Fukuda: As I listened to you, a question that I have long had comes across my mind. That is, whether it wasn't the result of the U.S. effort to force American-style democracy on Vietnam that the country became undemocratic.

We can say the U.S. put up Ngo Dinh Diem and pulled him down. Then the U.S. put up Nguyen Cao Ky and pulled him down again. Since South Korea allows a certain degree of authoritarian government—I don't think it is a dictatorship—and a strong one, they are doing fairly well as we can see. What do you think?

Passin: I am not defending the U.S. I am only trying to

explain why I think it has changed so much.

Muramatsu: A large number of American Senators and Congressmen have visited Vietnam and South Korea. Qualitatively, South Korea is quite different from Vietnam. With the exception of Hue, South Vietnam had had neither experience in nation building nor a viable bureaucracy. The educational standard wasn't worth mentioning.

Compared with South Vietnam, South Korea is not favored climatically, but she is a nation which has striven in this adverse climate. Her cultural tradition is time-honored; her educational standard is high. The problem is her all-to-brief experience with national administration. As the Yi dynasty (1392—1910) did not adopt feudalism, aristocracy persisted and weakened the basis of the nation. I don't want to use the term dictatorship. But with the enemy only 40Km away from the capital city, and survival of the nation foremost in the thoughts of the Korean people, it is inevitable that they acquiesce to some extent in authoritarianism. I think the United States is unaware of the distinctions between South Korea and South Vietnam.

Passin: In Japan, too, no distinction is made between the two. When I read Japanese newspapers and listen to what the intellectuals are saying, I conclude that there is not much difference between the U.S. and Japan in this regard.

Muramatsu: That may be so. But in the case of Japan the response of the press differs a little from that of the general public. In America, the difference between them is . . .

Passin: Here, I should point out one thing. As far as the human rights issue is concerned, Japanese newspapers press for vigorous implementation of American policy while they do not report any news about what is happening inside Vietnam or in Cambodia where hundreds of thousands of people have been massacred or killed. They also have not reported the terrorism in Laos. And obviously they do not report these things in China.

By this I do not mean to say that Japanese journalists lack a social conscience but simply that when it comes to the question of South Korea, this conscience is suddenly aroused. They say they have found gross violations of human rights there. In Korea, from 100 to 200 political prisoners are reportedly in jail. How many political prisoners are there in North Korea? How many would there be if anyone had the courage to speak up? It is certainly wrong for a government to infringe upon the rights of its citizens. But, it is very important to apply the same yardstick to both parts of the peninsula, not simply to the south. And this Japanese journalism, on the whole, fails to do.

Let me take an example. To protest strongly against South Korea, but not against Cambodia, Vietnam, Laos, Ethiopia, North Korea, the Soviet Union, and China— this is immoral. Provincial and even primitive as it may be, President Carter's moralism is far better than this.

Fukuda: You're right! But Mr. Carter himself is not as critical of the Japanese press as we are in our book, *Shinbun no subete* (All About the Press). He doesn't know much about Japanese pressdom, but he overrates Japan. Such poor, excessive morality is embarrassing indeed.

Muramatsu: Generally, the attitude of the Japanese papers is abnormal. Even if they perceive a situation correctly, they don't print it as is perceived.

Passin: It's very curious, but there's nothing we can do about it. It's commercialism.

Muramatsu: Generally, the American newspapers are not as harsh as their counterparts in Japan.

Passin: They are not as uniform in tone as the Japanese newspapers are.

Wakamatsu: Vietnam differs from South Korea in many ways, and the greatest difference is the outlook the Vietnamese and the South Koreans have on their states. Were the South Vietnamese really conscious that theirs was a sovereign nation? What will and determination did they have to defend their own country?

But in South Korea, the people have a keen spirit of nationalism and have a clear consciousness that they should defend and preserve their own country. I think it necessary for the United States to clearly distinguish between a country that has a will to defend herself and one that doesn't. Help should be given the former.

Passin: I quite agree. In the United States, I have always stressed this point. But this is only my opinion. Many Americans disagree with me. In Japan, too, many people oppose this view, I think.

Wakamatsu: The keener the belief of the South Koreans that they should defend their country themselves and the more Korean politicians are imbued with this sense of mission, the likelier South Korea comes to accept the harsh circumstances she faces—what the Japanese mass media likes to term "dictatorship" or "repression of freedom." Before we criticize South Korea, we should put ourselves in her place and think what we would do if we were in the position of South Korean politicians under these circumstances. It is my impression that the South Korean Government is acting rather diffidently, timidly looking around to see what moves other countries might make.

On the other hand, on the other side of the Military Demarcation Line, North Korea is enforcing a thoroughgoing news blackout that can never compare with what South Korea has and suffers a dictatorship that is far more stringent than in China, and Soviet Russia.

Well, many Japanese who have been to North Korea say—and the Japanese mass media play it up—that the country is free, that when they shook hands with Kim Il Sung, his hand felt soft or that they were honored to have seen so great a leader. But, they condemn on one pretext or another trials conducted in the South Korean courts. To South Korea, this is nothing short of intervention in her internal affairs. This constitutes an injustice to South Korea.

The curious position of Professor Reischauer

Kase: To say that the United States defends South Korea for the defense of Japan is to give a slap-in-the-face to the Korean people. On reflection, we see that the U.S. was responsible for division of the Korean Peninsula, for making Korea a divided country. Unlike the partition of Germany into the east and the west, the United States generously ceded the northern part of the peninsula to Soviet Russia.

To do justice to the United States, however, South Korea sent her troops to Vietnam, troops which fought valiantly.

Our feeling is that even if President Carter is to advocate moral diplomacy, he should apply an appropriate standard to South Korea.

Passin: I admit that the United States has made many mistakes including, among others, the division of Korea and Germany. But it isn't true that the United States handed the northern part of the Korean Peninsula to the Soviet Union out of sheer naiveté. The fact is that the Soviet Union was physically present there. This is not just a question of the Soviet troops invading the north in the last few days of the Second World War. The Soviet Union borders North Korea and there was no way the United States could keep the Russians from entering. Given the political naiveté of the United States at that time, it was lucky that the whole peninsula wasn't handed over to the Soviets.

Also, remember that it was the American troops that occupied Japan after the war and thus kept the Soviets from setting foot on Japanese soil.

The Soviet Union wanted very much to come into Japan. It offered to occupy Hokkaido, and some Allied powers supported the idea. But General MacArthur turned them down.

But in Korea, as in Germany, the Soviets were already present. The problem there was where the advancing Russians were to be halted. So, it isn't quite fair to hold the U.S. entirely responsible for the division of these countries. Nor is it correct historically.

Kase: No, I don't think so. At that time, the United States had little interest in the Korean Peninsula. We can see that in the policies pursued by the U.S. military government in Korea.

That no distinction is made between Vietnam and Korea may in part be attributed to the American people's ignorance. But if we were to transfer the issue of the withdrawal of the American troops in Korea to the European scene, Americans would find it hard to propose the withdrawal of some 300,000 American ground troops or the tactical nuclear weapons deployed there. Isn't there a tendency, after all, to stress Europe, to slight Asia, and to think lightly of South Korea?

Passin: That's a bit exaggerated. But, at the hearings I referred to before, I said what you've just said: It is insulting to say that we defend South Korea only for the defense of Japan; we should defend South Korea for her own sake.

The argument that the defense of Korea is necessary for the defense of Japan derives from two considerations. First, people who oppose the withdrawal of U.S. troops from Korea used this argument as a new second line of defense to fall back on while trying to reverse the Korea-withdrawal policy.

Many people want the United States to withdraw completely from Korea. They say that the United States shouldn't care about what happens on the Korean Peninsula since it does not involve our vital national interest. Perhaps we could call this a neo-Achesonian doctrine.

Therefore, those who favor the defense of South Korea have retreated to the position that even if Korea is not important for itself it is very important for the defense of Japan. This is a position that gets wider public support since many Americans still favor the defense of Japan, even though they may not be sure about South Korea. For myself, however, this is not only wrong but downright disgusting.

The second consideration is the view of many Japanese that stability in northeast Asia is more important than who will be the master of the Korean Peninsula. While some Americans hold this nonsensical position, it has been reinforced by a large number of Japanese. This Japanese view is in turn conveyed individually to Americans or spread through the medium of the press.

At a meeting in New York about a year ago at the Council on Foreign Relations, I heard people opposed to South Korea say grudgingly: "If an American presence in Korea is necessary for the defense of Japan, OK, but not for the defense of South Korea."

Fukuda: Then why doesn't someone stand up and ask clearly why Japan is so important as to be allowed the status of a security freeloader? (*Laughter*.)

Kase: Last year, Professor Reischauer testified before the same subcommittee that Mr. Passin did. He spoke to the effect that even if the Korean Peninsula were communized Japan would adroitly inure herself to it. I have a copy of the letter Professor Reischauer wrote to Mr. Donald M. Fraser (Chairman of the Subcommittee on International Organizations and Movements of the Foreign Relations Committee of the House), which is identical in content to his testimony. He argues that a communized Korea would not affect Japan since a wide strait separates the two countries. This is the first reason given.

Another reason cited is that a majority of Japan's neighbors are already communist countries and that the Japanese have grown accustomed to living with them. So the American troops in Korea that are held in hostage at present can be withdrawn without damaging Japanese confidence in the United States.

Muramatsu: Another thing is not to lose face.

Kase: That's true. If they don't lose face, they can withdraw. This is what Professor Reischauer testified.

Passin: I do not happen to agree with Professor Reischauer on this matter, so I am not trying to defend him. (*Laughter.*) But, as for the conclusions he has drawn, I think, Japan itself is partly responsible. Judging from what the Japanese mass media are now saying, this is not at all a strange conclusion for him to have drawn.

Japan should give a little thought to its own responsibility and that of journalism. The fact is that on many issues it is not only Professor Reischauer but other influential Americans who take their cues from the Japanese mass media. "If the Japanese don't think it matters whether we stay in Korea or not, why should we?" many people feel.

People often point out that there is a gap between the press and the public, and this is probably true. But the foreigners interested in Japan pay attention not only to what the government says but to what the Japanese press reports. In most cases, the press report is the more influential, and official announcements by the government are regarded with suspicion. Americans meet Japanese from many different spheres with many different views. So they end up never quite sure what the Japanese position is.

Kase: Had the press been Japan's spokesman, Japan might have already gone to ruin. I'd like to point out now what Professor Reischauer is saying in short: "The Japanese are worthy of defense but not the Koreans."

Love-hate relationship between Japan and America

Fukuda: By now, this point has been discussed several times. To raise it anew, the United States wouldn't make such rude remarks to Europe as she does to South Korea. She cannot, and will not, say that the defense of West Germany is not for its own sake, but is necessary for the defense of England, France or Europe in general.

As I have said already, to say to Asians that the defense of Vietnam is for the sake of South Korea and the defense of South Korea is for the sake of Japan is to show disrespect for the human rights of Asian peoples. To Mr. Carter, the Negroes are more important than Asians. They made him President. (*Laughter*.) Let's set aside this matter. But if we apply this logic, the next question that arises is why Japan is to be defended.

Passin: I think the Japanese tend to look down on other Asian people. They think they are superior and they do not trouble to hide their contempt. The attitude is easily detected and it arouses a lot of hostility.

In general, it is true that the United States is interested in Europe. The principal reason is strategic, not simply prejudice or traditional ties. I think that an emphasis on Europe to the detriment of Asia is strategically incorrect and when people realize it, the United States' attitude will swing back a bit. The reason the pendulum has swung so far this time is basically the Vietnam war. Americans lost confidence in the position they had held until then, and the demand for the withdrawal is linked to isolationism and other ideological considerations and is not confined only to Asia.

The isolationist begins with Asia because he finds it easier to be convincing there as a result of the bitter experiences of the Vietnam war. When the opportunity presents itself, he will not hesitate to press for withdrawal from Europe.

Therefore, I don't think any racial, geographical, or other prejudices are in themselves responsible. The argument for withdrawal is mistaken, but to the isolationist it is easier to start with Asia.

Kase: Ambassador Mansfield is one who thinks that way.

Muramatsu: What a big shot for an ambassador! (*Laughter.*)

Fukuda: We are thrown into despair now. We can no longer do anything about the so-called Japanese-American "connection."

Passin: The ambassador has felt that way for a long time. He has from time to time proposed that the U.S. should also withdraw from Europe. But President Carter certainly doesn't think so.

Kase: I regret to say that I still think there are some racial considerations behind the withdrawal from Asia.

Fukuda: It's the minority view that calls for withdrawal from Europe.

Passin: Yes, but some people do demand that.

Fukuda: But the majority supports the disengagement from South Korea.

Passin: Not necessarily so. Considering Congressional reaction, which is usually a good indication of public opinion, I am not at all sure that is the case.

Fukuda: Aside from the Congress, public opinion in the United States doesn't recognize South Korea or Taiwan as states.

Passin: That's something of an overstatement. South

Korea has behaved very badly. In the very midst of the debate on troop withdrawal, the KCIA (Korean Central Intelligence Agency) influence-buying scandal crops up. At the very least, that was very poor timing.

Fukuda: Wrongful as it is, there also is the Lockheed scandal in Japan. America could have thrown out such a premodern country for good. But this has not aroused distrust of Japan. Then, why is it that Japan should be defended even if South Korea is forsaken?

Passin: That's not quite the same thing. There are two things to consider about the KCIA influence-buying scandal. First it has more repercussions than the Lockheed scandal because it was an attempt to corrupt the U.S. Congress. Second, the Congressmen involved have not yet admitted their involvement. The whole business makes the U.S. Congress look very bad, so the repercussions are far greater among the people.

Kase: I read in *Time* or *Newsweek* that the KCIA began doling out money in the United States Congress in 1971 when the 20,000-man 7th Infantry Division of the United States Army was withdrawn from Korea. As no consultations had been made with South Korea in advance, it caused a panic in the country. Another point was that South Korea had distributed the money rather awkwardly.

I think that not only South Korea but many other countries were using lobbyists and were perhaps distributing gift-wrapped money to American Congressmen. So I should say that South Korea simply did it clumsily and that the United States was responsible for driving South Korea to go to such an extreme.

Passin: As for the United States' responsibility, I think the weakened leadership of the president is much to blame, and I am sorry that that is the case.

Fukuda: It may be repetitious, but I am most curious to know why Japan is valued so highly. Unless the reason is given clearly for this, future Japanese-American as well as American-Asian relations will not work smoothly.

Let me return to the point mentioned a little while ago that the Five-Year Modernization Plan of the South Korean armed forces hasn't gone well even with United States assistance. If we put ourselves in the place of South Korea, we can easily see that President Park has concentrated his efforts on the stabilization of people's living, on economic development and on the improvement of the consumers' life while the American troops are maintained in Korea. On the basis of the American military presence, he may have slowed down the tempo of the modernization of the South Korean armed forces.

And isn't this true of Japan? Japan has become an economic giant because as a security freeloader she has been able to well-nigh neglect her defense. "You say Japan is an independent country, but you do nothing to defend your own country. America will not care even if you are attacked. We will simply withdraw from Japan." Why doesn't the United States say this to Japan? Ever since the days of American occupation, Japan has been a country which can do nothing and can't see anything for herself unless the United States gives her one direction or another. (*Laughter.*)

Passin: In the U.S., this view is present. It is not held by many, but recently it has been gaining strength.

Fukuda: The voice should be raised loud enough to make it heard in Japan and to make Japan reflect upon herself. The United States should not bully such weak nations as South Korea—please excuse my rude expression. She would do better bully such developed major powers as Japan. Then it will become clear for the first time where the United States stands vis-a-vis Asia, and conversely, where Asia stands in relation to the United States.

Passin: There are more people in the U.S. who feel this way too.

Muramatsu: Isn't that an indication of ambivalence?

Passin: Yes, of course.

Muramatsu: Once the United States is gone, Japan will strengthen her military power and have her own way. If Japan goes nuclear, its impact on the United States will be far greater than that of the nuclear armament of India. It will be embarrassing to the United States. So she wants Japan to be kept in the present condition with her actual, not psychological, military power pegged at present strength. On the other hand, she feels that Japan should brace herself up. This places the United States in an ambivalent position vis-a-vis Japan.

Passin: There certainly is ambivalence in America thinking about Japan's defense. While we want Japan to assume a larger defense burden, we don't want her to become too strong. Because of this ambivalence, we continue to pay a high price to keep American troops in Japan. The same thing can be said about political relations. However, this ambivalence also results from a kind of love-hate attitude on the part of the Japanese and from the politically conflicting statements about the U.S.-Japan relationship that we are always getting from different parts of Japan's political spectrum.

This makes it hard for Americans to comprehend what Japan's real position is.

In this sense, the contradictory positions or attitudes manifested by the U.S. derive fundamentally from Japan's own vagueness.

Fukuda: Isn't this also true of South Korea? Does the United States think she won't go nuclear?

Muramatsu: Perhaps America thinks South Korea can't. She is probably underrating South Korea's potential on this

38

point.

Fukuda: As far as defense is concerned, today's Japan is insignificant—when compared with the United States—since she has been hamstrung in the past thirty years. It will take another thirty years or so for Japan to come to maturity in this field.

Kase: When I went to the United States last year and again this year, I met some officials at the White House and the Pentagon. They complained that one percent of GNP isn't enough for Japan's military budget. When I asked what percentage they thought would be enough, they preferred around two percent. I told them since Japan is spending less than one percent, she has been left far behind. Then I suggested 4-5 percent, instead of 2 percent, to enable Japan to make real headway. My American friends opposed this on the ground that it would tip the balance in Asia.

Well, let's look at the postwar United States policy toward Germany. America is asking Germany to arm herself to the fullest possible degree. Presumably the United States feels at ease with her since the West German troops are under the command of NATO. Not to make the same request of Japan which is also a defeated country must be the result of America's inbred mistrust of Japan.

Also, America is probably reckoning that as long as Japan depends on America for defense, she can have a docile Japan at her beck and call.

Is America trustworthy?

Passin: As I said just now, there is no doubt that there is in the U.S. some distrust of Japan. An ambivalence does exist as Mr. Muramatsu has remarked.

Muramatsu: Americans may say, to take an example, "Carry on with your efforts to defend the Tsushima Strait, but don't go beyond that." (*Laughter.*) In short, America wants Japan to play the role of an auxiliary.

Fukuda: I know many different voices are raised in America, but the question is which represents the general drift of opinion, or which is the loudest voice.

Passin: But public opinion does change. We are now in a very volatile period. Things may turn about completely.

Fukuda: Could there be a change in the policy of withdrawal?

Passin: While matters are not yet entirely clear, I would say yes, there can be a change. During the next five years ahead, there might very easily be changes in the situation that would force the U.S. to stop the withdrawal very far short of completion. Right now the Administration gives the appearance of being determined to complete the withdrawal for reasons of domestic U.S. politics. But many people are very skeptical about the desirability of complete withdrawal, so it's doubtful how far the Administration can go.

Kase: Any extension of internal politics should not become an expediency which affects the security problem of Northeast Asia.

Passin: The foreign policy of any country is linked to its internal politics. The studied ambiguity of many official statements of the Japanese Government, for example, are clearly related to domestic political considerations.

Muramatsu: That's right! As far as this matter is concerned, Japan's behavior is most outrageous. America should not take cue from Japan. (*Laughter*.)

Passin: The Executive Branch in the U.S. has lost much of its power. There are two reasons for this. First, the defeat in Vietnam, which seriously eroded public confidence in the Administration. Second, the Watergate scandal, which only reinforced this lack of confidence. This is a reality that cannot be disregarded. In the past, this was not the case. Hopefully, the Executive will be able to recover a better balance with the Legislative. We are now, as I have said before, in a transition period. It is still necessary to move very slowly, because of domestic constraints on foreign policy. And this is true of Japan also.

Kase: Mr. Passin said America was defeated in Vietnam. But the most serious problem of the Vietnam war was that America lost the will to fight. And so Vietnam went down the river. It might have been better, had the United States been defeated militarily. But she simply lost her will to fight. This is the greatest tragedy.

Wakamatsu: It gave a direct shock to South Korea. Had American tactics or strategy been faulty in Vietnam, criticisms would be directed only at those military flaws. The United States had long and loudly proclaimed, on the strength of the domino theory, that the whole of Southeast Asia would go if Vietnam went. But then Congress coolly refused the 350 million dollars that Vietnam had requested and so urgently needed to turn the tide of the war. When America declared that she had given up the fight, those who felt the greatest impact were none other than the Korean people, not the Vietnamese who should have been the ones to feel it. After witnessing what might have been a vivid test case in Vietnam, the South Koreans must have felt that America might also ditch them any time she felt it convenient to do so.

Fukuda: You've said it! As Mr. Kase mentioned before, 1971 saw the withdrawal of an American infantry division comprising 20,000 personnel, and in October of that year, President Park proclaimed a state of emergency. In a sense, we can attribute this to the Vietnam shock. President Park was at a loss to know how far he could trust America and was thus driven into taking such action.

Muramatsu: Because the event was preceded by the

announcement of the Guam Doctrine. And in 1972 the Korean constitution was amended.

Fukuda: Another thing I'd like to talk about is the deployment of American ground troops halfway between the Demilitarized Zone and Seoul. Rumor has it—though its authenticity has not been confirmed—that President Park once recommended to the Americans that they move their troops southward, down to Pusan, because their presence in the north might provoke North Korea. But the American troops insisted on going to the frontline. This resulted in that unfortunate "Poplar Tree Incident."[3] Now, the United States is withdrawing these troops from Korea. Thus the South Koreans think that the Americans are acting too arbitrarily.

Kase: One more thing about America's arbitrary action. Under some circumstances, it becomes unavoidable to restrict freedoms in order to protect them. This is often done in democratic countries. For example, during the Algerian crisis, France gave dictatorial powers to De Gaulle. In the case of Mr. Passin's country, the United States, President Lincoln arrested and imprisoned several thousand people without warrants of arrest during the Civil War. During the Second World War, American citizens of Japanese ancestry were sent to concentration camps. America does restrict freedoms in time of national crisis.

I think that among the developing nations South Korea is a very free country. The Philippines is under martial law, and there are no Congresses or opposition parties. Such anti-government papers as the *Manila Times* have gone out of existence. In Korea, the National Assembly does exist. So do troublesome opposition parties and anti-government papers like the *Dong-A Ilbo*. If you simply stand on a street corner in

---

3. In August 1976, a melee took place between the United States soldiers trying to trim the poplar tree and North Korean security guards in Panmunjom. The fighting resulted in the killing of two American officers.

42

South Korea watching people, you will not fail to see how free the country is.

What is important for a developing country is, first of all, economic growth. Today, the promotion of the people's living standard has become the most important South-North issue throughout the world. Economic activities call for social stability which in turn depends upon the existence of political stability. Among developing countries, South Korea is outstanding. We hear that her way of doing things is poor or that the death penalty should not have been demanded for poet Kim Chi Ha—though he ultimately got a life sentence. But, fundamentally, South Korea is a free country among developing nations.

Passin: I agree with what you have said. Both Japan and the U.S. should think about the outstanding progress South Korea is making.

Let me emphasize that we are not talking only about the American attitude. Just read the Japanese newspapers if you want to see real on fairness. Although I mentioned this earlier, let me come back to it again.

Many Japanese criticize the "excesses" of South Korea, but keep completely silent about North Korea. Some journalists defend themselves by saying that there is no way to know what is going on in North Korea. This very statement itself reveals a lack of balance in reporting. They divide events into those they are willing to check into and those they are not. The very structure of the situation reveals their prior bias. When they look at the south, they look for defects; when they look at the north, they don't try to find defects on the grounds that they are forbidden to do so. And in this basis they end up with the conclusion—or at least giving the reader the impression—that the south suppresses freedom and the north does not.

Certainly freedoms are constrained in South Korea.

About 150 persons are currently in jail for political reasons, though they are not all receiving the same kind of treatment. But in North Korea, political dissent cannot be expressed in any form. Even were a dissenter to try to shout his views to the outside world, nobody would even hear it.

In the U.S., we are opposed to the kind of double standard that is so often found among leftwing liberals. But in Japan, this double standard has become the rule. The name Kim Chi Ha has become a household word among the Japanese. This is not because he was a famous and beloved poet, but only because the left, with the help of commercial journalism, has succeeded in making it a symbol of freedom resisting oppression. How many thousands of silent oppressed have they simply neglected to notice in the north.

My question, then, is not why this is not understood by Americans, but why it is not understood by Japanese.

U.S. slights Asia

Uncertainty of the American commitment to defend Japan

Fukuda: A little while ago, Mr. Passin said the foreign
policy of all countries is related to their internal politics. That's
quite true.

But there was once a time when America took upon herself the role of, or was expected to be, the policeman of the
world. Is America different from other countries? Shouldn't
she take pride in that?

At the same time, when the U.S. advocates moral diplomacy or human rights diplomacy, she is assigning herself—
to put it sarcastically—the role, not of world policeman, but
of the judge, missionary Redeemer of the world. (*Laughter*.)
It's more pompous.

If I interpret it perversely, being the policeman requires
money, but playing the missionary doesn't. So I think it is the
slogan that has changed, not the consciousness of being the
leader of the free world. In America, I mean.

Muramatsu: The trouble is that Carter the Baptist missionary has no sense of responsibility as I said before.

Fukuda: That's right! Therefore, America should re-
frain, more than any other country, from using diplomacy as a

tool of internal politics. America has pride and power. She should be more principled than Japan, the European countries and others including South Korea in pursuing foreign policies that may be construed as a tool of internal politics. We place so much expectation in her.

Passin: That involves many difficult problems. Under some circumstances, the insistence on human rights is unavoidable or necessary. For example, we should help the Jewish people in the Soviet Union as well as the intellectuals in Eastern Europe. This is very difficult to do, but the consequences of not doing so are too serious.

The Japanese people have a convenient habit of not seeing what goes on under their very eyes. Look at the way they treat Vietnamese refugees. I must confess that I cannot help getting furious about this kind of thing.

Thousands of people escaped from Vietnam in tiny unseaworthy boats that could not survive in the open seas. These people risked being caught by the Vietnamese navy or starving to death. They fled the Communist "paradise" at the risk of their lives on the outside chance that they might be found and rescued by friendly ships.

And when some of them were picked up by a Japanese or a Japan-bound ship and did arrive in Japan, they were treated like sub-human beings or unclaimed baggage and are denied entry. I think this is immoral indeed. Where do we draw the line between moral diplomacy and realistic diplomacy—the problem is difficult but it is not disposed of by throwing human rights overboard.

Fukuda: You have said such charming things. (*Laughter.*)

Passin: As you have all argued, Carter may be going about things in the wrong way, but I think and hope he has learned from his mistakes.

Muramatsu: Once I saw a map of the world showing the

latitude of freedom. It was published by a certain research institute in Europe. The countries judged by common sense to be generally free were shown in white while those in which there was no freedom were shown in black. Between them were countries shown in two gradations of grey: The lesser the freedom, the darker the color and the greater the freedom, the lighter the color.

The only Asian country shown in white was Japan. Also painted white were some countries in Europe; the United States and Canada on the American continent, and New Zealand and Australia. Surprisingly, there were one or two white spots in Africa—Kenya or other places like that.

Naturally, such Communist countries as China, Soviet Russia and North Korea were in black. The rest of the countries, the so-called Third World countries, in shades of grey.

If we carry human rights diplomacy to an extreme, we will finally have to declare war against the Communist camp. This is not because a dictator has haphazardly come into being, but because no Communist countries recognize freedom as its cardinal national policy. If the Central Committee of the Communist Party of a Communist country allows freedom of speech to those who have been declared counter-revolutionary or reactionary elements, that country will no longer be a Communist one. Not to recognize freedom is the cardinal national policy of any Communist country. If we are determined to clash head-on with such a country, therefore, we should attack the policy. This would be tantamount to a declaration of war. Such is the natural consequence of logic.

Let me take another instance, that of President Amin of Uganda. African countries don't approve of his methods. But, if America brings her full pressure to bear on Amin, these same African countries will rise in his defense, linking the American pressure to the issue of racial prejudice. America cannot act high-handedly against any country which infringes on human rights. Moral diplomacy is effective only with regard to America's allies.

Wakamatsu: The United States is forcing human rights diplomacy upon those within her sphere of influence.

Muramatsu: America remains silent over the bloody purges in China, but grumbles about the Philippines. She holds her tongue about the hereditary dynasty emerging in North Korea while she reproaches South Korea. Human rights diplomacy serves only to weaken the governments of America's allies.

Passin: I don't like this any better than you do. But, it is not confined to the U.S.; if anything, it is even more prevalent in Japan.

To some extent this may be traced to those who favor closer freindship with the Soviet Union. We demand, perhaps out of a Puritanical strain or out of naive moralism, that our allies respect human rights. But we feel there is nothing we can do about those who are not our friends, much less who are our enemies. We know our enemies are wrong. Therefore, we don't expect anything of them and we can't do anything about it. But we expect our friends to do better.

The Japanese manage to make themselves look very moral on the cheap. The cost is very low. You can criticize a friendly country with impunity but not a Communist country or a developing nation; they will hit back.

Israel, for example, will not retaliate no matter how unfairly she may be treated. In fact to denounce Israel may bring some benefit from the Arabs. But if the suppression of freedom in an Arab state were denounced, as it is in South Korea, the flow of oil or trade relations might suffer. Thus there is every reason for Japan to cringe before a totalitarian or dictatorial country. The result is a very sordid imbalance. If you want a good example, just see how little space is given by the Japanese media to the news about the massacres now taking place in Laos and Cambodia(Note: The situations has changed somewhat since the time this was written.)

Kase: As Assistant Secretary of State Richard Holbrooke testified at a hearing conducted by the United States Congress, it is estimated that some 1,200,000 Cambodians have been killed since their country was communized. It's terrifying! Cambodia's population is only 7 million.

Fukuda: Japan is a major exception. No country which has studied her would enter into a security pact with her. She isn't qualified to sign a military treaty. Since Japan does not strive to defend herself, no country would sign such a treaty with her.

Therefore, I began to wonder several years ago why Japan is fondled so much and whether there is any hidden motive for this. If there be any motive, it must be that America defends Japan because she needs her. That is what the leftists are saying. It is reasonable to say more simply that America defends Japan because she needs the Japanese market. We have all been thick-and-thin pro-Americans. But now we find it hard to defend our position. We are even inclined to think that what the leftists are saying is true.

Wakamatsu: Mr. Fukuda compared South Korea with Europe. If I go to an extreme, Europe is an end to America whereas Asia provides a means. America now defends Asia as a means while her real end is the security of Europe.

Fukuda: Asia is the postern for defending the front gate. Some will deny this, but I absolutely believe it. I am not biased. To be fair, I only hope they will appreciate the importance of the postern.

Wakamatsu: Now, Japan is an end in Asia. America defends South Korea as a means of defending Japan. But as time goes by, Japan may become a means, too.

Fukuda: I think Japan is already a means.

Wakamatsu: There undoubtedly is a fear or anxiety

about that. The fact is that South Korea, while professing to trust America, inwardly strongly distrusts her and is experiencing great uncertainty.

Fukuda: She doesn't trust America at all.

Muramatsu: A Korean saying goes, "Don't be deceived by Soviet Russia. Don't trust America."

Wakamatsu: At present, South Korea cannot defend herself without Japan. This plight will continue for some time to come. In that sense, South Korea is unfortunate indeed.

Fukuda: America says, as Mr. Wakamatsu remarked, that she defends South Korea in order to keep Japan secure. If the U.S. goes one step further and says the defense of Japan is for America or for Europe, then Japan becomes a means for preserving the security of America or Europe. We always fear that America will dump Japan unless the importance attached to this "means" is not fully recognized.

But there is no such uncertainty among most Japanese people because America has already implied that she will never give up Japan. Why? I have never been convinced that America is acting out of kindness. America allows Japan to be a security freeloader because she fears, as all of you have observed, that Japan will become a military superpower. This is a case of a burnt child who dreads the fire. On this point, the anti-establishment activists in Japan—for example the leftists or progressives represented by Hani Goro and Mukaizaka Itsuro—are like twin brothers of America. (*Laughter*.)

Passin: The U.S. and Japan should think seriously about this. Until recently, it has always appeared to people that it was the U.S. that was forcing the security treaty on a reluctant Japan. This is why the Japanese left opposes the treaty.

But, this is now a thing of the past. Today Americans are beginning to wonder why our troops continue to be stationed in Japan. The two countries should review this matter serious-

50

ly. Right now, it is my feeling that the shoe is on the other foot, Japan should be trying to persuade the U.S. rather than the other way around.

Muramatsu: One of the reasons that America needs Japan is to be assured of a base for the 7th Fleet. Another stems from her concern lest Japan's industrial capabilities be utilized by China or Soviet Russia.

Kase: Then the balance between East and West will be destroyed.

Muramatsu: When these two concerns have been allayed to some degree, the American troops could be withdrawn, couldn't they?

Passin: That's an important question.

Fukuda: With regard to the question of balance: If Japan chooses to side with China, rather than with Soviet Russia, the balance will tip in another direction, America committing herself only to Europe . . .

Muramatsu: If America comes to terms with China—setting aside the question of Soviet Russia—there will be no possibility that the technology of Japan, even if linked with Chinese manpower, will be turned against America. Further improvement of naval weaponry and the resulting change in the quality of naval forces will free the 7th Fleet from its dependence on Yokosuka, Sasebo and other bases.

Fukuda: America may draw back to the Mariana Islands, or to borrow the words of Mr. Nasu Hijiri, she may lease some Chinese ports. (*Laughter*.)

Wakamatsu: Some Americans support the idea of retreating to the Marianas. For several years now, studies have been made to determine the best place to build the new island base. As weaponry is developed, and it becomes no longer necessary to send troops directly as far as Northeast Asia,

American strategy may well change.

The air force can withdraw at any time

Muramatsu: A good naval port must meet some requirements: There must be a nearby industrial area and a nearby supply base to serve the ships. Without these, the importance of a port decreases.

Wakamatsu: Yes, it does, but only when a port doesn't boast these requirements to a certain degree. The 7th Fleet is already in the Western Pacific around Japan. Unlike the Russians, the Americans will not endure sea service for several months without break, so they need a base for rest and recuperation, supplies and overhauling. At present, only Japan provides such bases.

Muramatsu: For the time being, you mean.

Wakamatsu: So Japan is indispensable now. Besides those in Japan, there are other ports, of course. But none have such excellent facilities for rest and recuperation of naval personnel and for supplying and overhauling of ships. America has decided to continue to station her air and naval forces in South Korea. She prefers to reinforce the air force there. Her combat vessels will continue to call frequently at South Korean ports. Conversely, however, while such forces may move to Korea now, and even be supplemented, these forces can also withdraw at any time. The air force could be reinforced promptly and markedly. If so desired; scores of planes could be thrown into Korea. But a change of mind could result in the sudden withdrawal of all of them. (*Laughter*.)

Muramatsu: Because they are winged.

Wakamatsu: The same thing can be said about ships. Americans say their air and naval forces will remain in Korea, but is this certain? They say that their ground troops will be phased out in five years; the money and weapons being transferred to Korea during the period, that American troops will be withdrawn only after the South Korean armed forces have become strong enough to defend their country. When all the American soldiers are gone, South Korea—however strong she may have become by then—will find it hard to wage a lengthy lone war against North Korea, a country that has the backing of China and Soviet Russia. Since China shares a border with North Korea, she can pour her troops across the Yalu into North Korea just as she did during the Korean War. Even if America decides to recommit her ground forces, these cannot reach Korea for a long time. Should a war break out and should America decide not to involve herself on the pretense that she had adequately strengthened South Korea, another Vietnam might well be the result. Though she is carrying out a Forces Improvement Plan with modern weapons supplied or to be supplied by America, South Korea is deeply worried about the complete withdrawal of the American ground troops.

America may feel that in case of war she won't abandon South Korea. If she really feels that way, America should leave at least a token ground force on the peninsula. It's absolutely nonsensical even to talk about redeploying ground troops for Europe, as is reported in some papers.

Muramatsu: According to the *Military Balance* published by the International Institute for Strategic Studies in England, North Korea has 7,500 guns of various types and 680 rocket launchers. South Korea has about 2,500 pieces. The distance between Seoul and the Military Demarcation Line is only 40 Km. Protective mine fields can easily be neutralized by North Korea's densely concentrated artillery batteries. Moreover, there is a great gap between the south and the north in terms of warplanes, as has been already mentioned.

Wakamatsu: North Korea has a 3 to 1 numerical edge in

combat aircraft.

Muramatsu: South Korea has only half as many tanks as North Korea. North Korea has some 2,000 and produces about 100 a year.

North Korea does not intend to take the whole of the south, only Seoul and its environs. South Korea's total population stands somewhere between 32,000,000 to 33,000,000. Of this number, about 14,000,000 live in the metropolitan area. As with the population, a very large number of factories are concentrated in this area. If the North Koreans take Seoul in a short time, the south, having lost half of her population and industry, will be almost empty. This means that the south will be literally finished. So there's no need for invading the entire south. The north could take the Seoul area and make it a *fait accompli.* In other words, the north has an ideal target under its nose.

Kase: An Arab-Israeli type war may develop. When major powers intervene and achieve a cease-fire arrangement, the side which has taken territory becomes the victor in that short war.

Wakamatsu: In case of war between Israel and Egypt the result may be that the Suez Canal or the Mitlah Pass in the desert will be taken by one side or the other. But South Korea is different. If Seoul, 40 to 50 Km from the Military Demarcation Line, falls into hostile hands, South Korea will have lost her symbol and her national power. Even if left alone, the remainder of Korea will be absolutely powerless.

Originally, South Korea and America took different positions regarding the defense of Seoul. From a pure military point of view, America mapped out a strategy of giving up Seoul at the first strike from the north, of retreating south of the Han River there to build a strong defense line and then to strike back, and retake Seoul. On the other hand, South Korea took the position that since Seoul is the symbol and heart of South Korea, its fall would mean the loss of all of the country. Therefore, it was imperative that Seoul not be allowed to fall into enemy hands, that it be defended to the last. Korea announced her determination to adhere to this strategy even if it proved disadvantageous or irrational from the military viewpoint.

Regarding the defense of Seoul, then, the United States and South Korean viewpoints collided but the U.S. eventually conceded and agreed to defend Seoul. Now, the area between the Military Demarcation Line and Seoul is covered by the third to fifth lines of defense. Yet it is extremely difficult to defend enormously populated cities like Seoul. Once war comes, one of the greatest problems to be faced will be that of caring for and dealing with non-combatants. Should Seoul fall, it is difficult to imagine that America would come to South Korea's aid in retaking the capital city.

Muramatsu: Judging by common sense, that's unlikely to occur. Now, the United States 2nd Infantry Division and its anti-aircraft units do exist, and its M60 tanks total more than 100. These American troops are providing a deterrent. Basically, the presence of the American ground forces makes the American involvement inevitable in case of a North Korean invasion. But President Carter has said that he will withdraw the troops. Once these are withdrawn, there will be no guarantee that the air force will be committed. We have never seen that when ground troops are withdrawn the air force is thrown into combat.

Wakamatsu: Perhaps not. Even if the air force is committed, what effect do we expect?

Muramatsu: The same thing happened prior to the collapse of Vietnam. On the heels of the withdrawal of the American ground troops the North Vietnamese moved in violation of the Paris Agreement. Legally speaking, therefore, the United

States could have used her air force, but she didn't.

Kase: At that time, American combat planes were in Thailand. They stood idly by.

Muramatsu: The 7th Fleet was in the Philippines. Neither did it make any move. From these facts, we can say that once the American ground forces disappear from South Korea, there is no longer any guarantee that the American air force will be called out when North Korea unleashes a limited blitzkrieg.

And the problem is what deterrent South Korea by herself possesses. To North Korea, there is an ideal target of Seoul. Unless South Korea can strike back at a North Korean Achilles'heel in case Seoul is invaded, her deterrent power is useless. Bluntly, the north doesn't have any such weak point.

It won't be any better even if Pyongyang is captured. The north isn't an industrial country and its arsenals are mostly located underground. What South Korea can do is to destroy the North Korean troops themselves. South Korea isn't ready for that yet. This means that when the American troops are gone, South Korea will have no real deterrent at all.

"No threat from the north," a downright lie

Kase: The Carter Administration says that the withdrawal of the American ground troops won't weaken America's commitment to the defense of South Korea. But this assurance is a fragile one.

This reminds me that early in the Vietnam war the Kennedy Administration suddenly increased the number of American military advisers to 13,000 from the 600 men sent by the Eisenhower Administration. Then Under-Secretary of State William Bundy explained in his memoirs that the increase really didn't mean that there was any strengthening of the American commitment or involvement in the land warfare.

Now, the Americans say that their commitment to Korea won't be weakened. I think the reverse is the case.

Passin: I am opposed to the withdrawal of American ground troops from Korea. Nevertheless, I am, on the whole, rather optimistic about future developments.

First, South Korea is a very strong country and is becoming stronger every day. It is entirely capable of defending its freedom. North Korea is not so stupid as to take careless chances.

Second, the withdrawal is not going to be carried out all at once. It will be a long process lasting over five years. This means that at any time during this period—up to the very last moment—the process can be halted. Of course, this won't be easy. If a full commitment is made publicly, it should be honored whatever the difficulties in doing so. But I personally do not think this process will be carried out to the very end. There are many things that are likely to happen that will stop it well short of the final point.

I am sure that you have already noticed change in the tone of American newspapers and in the attitude of the American Senate. These are only further indications that American foreign policy is beginning to settle down on this question. On the whole, I am optimistic about this matter.

But, I am not optimistic about what Japan will do in the next five years.

Fukuda: Japan will do nothing unless she is spurred by America. But what happens if North Korea launches an attack within the five-year period, or rather during the tenure of President Carter? That will finish the political life of Mr. Carter.

Returning to what Messrs. Wakamatsu and Muramatsu have said, it may be possible to reason in the following way: The assessment that there is currently no threat of war from the north provides one of the major grounds for withdrawal of the American troops in Korea. But conversely speaking, they try to withdraw the troops since there is a threat from the north. As the threat of war becomes real, they are trying not to get involved in the war. The air force can get away quickly and the navy can keep itself in the distance. But the foot soldiers, if stationed, are bound to get involved and be held in hostage. So they thought it better to withdraw. I can reason in this way. Therefore, they may feel that they cannot be happy-go-lucky and leisurely withdraw American troops in five years. The pace of withdrawal may thus be accelerated beyond expectation.

Kase: That's what Professor Reischauer is saying.

Fukuda: It's strange to think that there isn't any threat from the north. North Korea is economically hard pressed or actually broke. Their only alternative may be to invade the south. I would do it if I were Kim Il Sung.

Muramatsu: There is also the problem of succession. Were I Kim Il Sung, I would do it, too.

Wakamatsu: We could think that way. As he is hard pressed economically and politically, he should crack down hard internally. One possibility is that he will become flexible externally in order to obtain foreign credits. Another possibility is that in despair, he will assume a rigid attitude in order to divert the attention of people outward. If internal repression reaches its limits, the north may adopt this sort of distracting strategy.

Muramatsu: By and large, this reasoning would be historically consistent.

Wakamatsu: There is also the problem of food shortage caused by poor crops. According to studies by meteorologists, the earth is becoming cooler. Some say we are entering a glacial age. Everywhere in the world, unusual meteorological phenomena have been observed. Under these circumstances, it will be possible for such agriculturally advanced countries as Japan to localize cold-weather damage and prevent it from developing into a great famine of national dimensions such as occurred in ancient times. They are also forced by economic considerations to buy food from abroad. However, the Korean Peninsula, as you know, is highly susceptible to the vagaries of weather, and drought is an ever-present problem on bald mountains.

Muramatsu: North Korea had that problem last year.

Wakamatsu: A drought, whether it is large or small in scope, always accompanies cold-weather damage. It is said that North Korea is building reservoirs of various sizes to impound water. They are effective during periods of drought, but are ineffective against cold-weather damage. Droughts and cold-weather damage, if they occur several years in a row, will result in a great famine causing severe food shortages.

In 1960, 1961 and 1962, North Korea fell prey to severe famines. As food became scarce, the people in the north had to peel off and pound the bark of trees for food. As a result, the trees in the mountains looked like white birches. An O Ki Wan, secretary to former Premier Kim Il, revealed this.

Muramatsu: That coincided with the famine in China.

Wakamatsu: Yes. If such a situation continued, North Korea might be driven to resort to a distracting high-wire act and invade the south because necessity knows no law.

Fukuda: That may be correct. And Kim Il Sung is always telling his people that the south should be unified by the north. He has repeated that again and again. Mindful of the people, he will be forced to resort to action in the end.

Wakamatsu: We should take that possibility into consideration. Besides, Kim Chong Il, a son of Kim Il Sung, is said to have been groomed as his successor. Although it's not clear why Kim Il Sung has had to choose his successor, I feel some sort of power struggle is going on in the inner circles in North Korea.

Muramatsu: Last year some leaders disappeared. All the seats of the 15-man Central Committee are taken up by pro-Kim Il Sung elements. No election was held, this in violation of the constitution.

Wakamatsu: Kim Il Sung is a man who has experienced the pains of revolution and of nation building. If a person without such experience assumes the dictatorship, he may run a risk. Kim Chong Il knows nothing of the world and may resort to adventurism. We cannot say definitely that there isn't any threat from the north. Threat of one sort or another does exist.

Kase: As already mentioned, South Korea has worked a miracle in economic growth. North Korea, on the other hand, is economically bankrupt. Her trade runs into red figures. She is unable to settle accounts externally.

And the economic gap is widening each year between the south and the north. This may drive North Korea to follow the suit of Japan which sought a way out of her desperation in the Second World War. So I think the premise is mistaken that another Korean War will not break out.

I heard from Gen. Richard Stilwell, who was the Commanding General of the American Forces in Korea up to the end of last year, that North Korea has the capability of waging war single-handedly up to four months. She has the war potential for that length of time.

We can make another assumption, paralleling the Arab-Israeli war. In 1973, Egypt crossed the Suez and launched a surprise attack on the Israelis on the Sinai peninsula. But at the last stage, the 3rd Army, the most treasured crack unit of Egypt, was encircled by the Israelis. However, it was saved by Soviet Russia just before it suffered a crushing blow. Similar-ly, even if North Korea failed in her venture, Soviet Russia would not let her go down the drain. Just as she saved Egypt's 3rd Army, she will no doubt intervene to save North Korea. If North Korea feels fairly assured of that, we cannot exclude the possibility that the north may have another fling at war. It's too optimistic to say that nothing is to be feared from North Korea because neither China nor Soviet Russia wants war.

War ruins everything

Passin: I quite agree. We can't say there isn't any threat. There are too many dangerous elements in the situation. Particularly important is the economic gap. The more North Korea envies the prosperous south, the more difficult it will be to manage her internal situation. There is danger that she may be tempted to divert internal pressure by some external adventure.

As I said already, I don't know what attitude Japan will take in the event that North Korea starts trouble. The use of U.S. bases in Japan will become a problem.

The opposition parties will certainly oppose their use. By then the Liberal Democratic Party Government may have become so weakened that it has to depend on a coalition to remain in office. The possibility is very high that the government will not feel itself secure enough to allow the U.S. to use the bases.

Another reason for Japanese hesitation about supporting U.S. military action is the possibility of a retaliatory attack or a strategic preemptive strike at Japan by North Korea and her allies—if she has any allies then. This fear tends to act as a restraint on the Japanese government.

Kase: That's a big question. The Korean War broke out in 1950 and ended in 1953. The war was still raging when the San Francisco Treaty was signed in April 1952, and Japan regained her independence. At that time, the Japan-U.S.

Security Agreement had no clause on advance consultations.

If another war were to break out, the U.S. should now consult Japan in advance. Even if the United States were allowed to use her bases in Japan, we will have to imagine what would follow then. Probably the Korean residents in Japan who support North Korea will demand that the Japanese Government withdraw the authorization to use American bases. Some radicals among them may go so far as to resort to Belfast-style terrorist tactics.

If a department store or a railway station is bombed and scores or hundreds of Japanese citizens are wounded or killed, the Japanese will hesitate to go through with their initial plan of helping the South Koreans defend themselves.

When the Korean War broke out in 1950, the United States military power was overwhelmingly strong, and China did not bomb Japan. Neither did North Korea attack Japan. But now, we cannot assume they won't venture to do so.

From the standpoint of international law, North Korea may invoke the right to hot pursuit if American warplanes make sorties from the bases in Japan. North Korean planes may pursue the American planes and bomb the bases in Japan, killing and wounding a large number of civilians around them. Then public opinion will become adversely affected and may question the wisdom of getting involved in the war at the sacrifice of Japanese people. Consequently, anti-war sentiment will pervade the whole country. Even today war is anathema to the Japanese.

If a war breaks out and America decides to defend South Korea as she has pledged to, her combat aircraft will have to make sorties from the bases in Japan. Likewise, the 7th Fleet will come into action. This means young Americans are to shed their blood for defense not of South Korea, but of Japan. Besides, public opinion in Japan will clamor vehemently against her involvement in the war as I've said already. This may undermine the Security Agreement itself.

In the long run, the pact will prove a dead letter or simply be scrapped. The Soviet Union which is currently requesting Japan to allow her to fish in Japan's territorial waters may then demand to let her hunt people in Japan's territory. (*Laughter*.) In case another Korean War breaks out, I think the most vulnerable nation in the free world will turn out to be Japan. Despite this, America is running a risk by withdrawing her ground combat troops in Korea that account for only one tenth of her troops stationed in Europe. We are quite puzzled to understand the reasons for this.

Passin: Therefore, I think that in the end the U.S. will decide not to withdraw.

Muramatsu: The South Korean troops stand totally on the defensive and have no credible deterrent power as I mentioned before. To make a deterrent work effectively, a country should have the structure and organization ready for production of tanks, armored personnel carriers, helicopters and other sophisticated weapons. It will take five to six years to produce them.

Kase: There are some preconditions that must be satisfied before the phase-out of the American troops in Korea. When the Armistice Agreement was concluded in 1953, the Communist side was represented by North Korea and China, and the other side by the Commander-in-Chief of the United Nations Forces. The representatives of these three governments signed the agreement, but South Korea didn't participate. How is this fundamental question to be dealt with? This is the question that must first be resolved prior to the withdrawal of the troops. Otherwise, the American ground troops will have gone without vesting South Korea with competency as a party to the Armistice Agreement. It's absurd!

Passin: I agree with you.

Wakamatsu: If the American troops are pulled out, one

party to the armistice talks will be missing as Mr. Kase pointed out. Imagine if a war breaks out and then talks start to stop it. As the South Korean representative takes a seat, the Communist side may say: "You are not entitled to sit there. The party qualified to sit there has gone. Without him, the Armistice Agreement is also gone." Thus the agreement becomes a scrap of paper.

Another problem is the five western islands including Paengnyon-do. These islands are located north of the seaward extension of the Military Demarcation Line and were placed under the jurisdiction of the United Nations Command by the Armistice Agreement. If the American ground troops are withdrawn, the United Nations Command no longer exists. So North Korea may lay claim to the islands and may venture to take them by force. The islands with radar screens are a thorn in the side of the north.

Muramatsu: Under the very nose of North Korea, the islands are keeping a close eye on every move the north makes in that area.

Five western islands in a touch-and-go situation

Wakamatsu: It's less than 20 Km from the Ongjin peninsula of North Korea to the nearest island. But the islands are 200 Km away from Kimpo Airport in South Korea.

The garrison there must be manned by a considerably large number of troops, but the problem is how to keep supplies going to them in case of a prolonged attack. In regard to defending islands, Japan had bitter experience during the Pacific War. Valiant as they were, the Japanese troops' fighting power was hamstrung and they were annihilated everywhere as they were cut off from supplies. We should know South Korea is now confronted with this serious problem.

Muramatsu: Furthermore, the airport there stands on

the sands. At high tide it is submerged. Only when the tide is out can planes land on the sandy beach. The tide rises and falls greatly, and the wide range of tide makes distribution of supplies very difficult.

Kase: These islands are fortified as Quemoy and Matsu are and reportedly can withstand a North Korean attack.

Wakamatsu: They cannot be taken as easily as a target on land because the islands are separated by a sea even though it is less than 20 Km wide. But they come well within the range of long-range guns. On the other hand, South Korea has to provide supplies only by planes and ships. So this will prove disadvantageous to South Korea as the days go by.

Kase: Recently, North Korea declared unilaterally a 200-mile military sea boundary extending well into the Yellow and Japan Seas. Some think the move was aimed at the western islands—a prelude to attempt a military venture there.

When I was in Korea some time ago, I was told that if the five western islands fall into the hands of North Korea, the prestige of the Park Chung Hee Government will be greatly marred, internally and externally. Therefore, South Koreans cannot let go of them under any circumstances.

If South Korea concludes that the islands are indefensible when the fighting is localized there, she may cross the 38th Parallel and escalate the war. Once the war is escalated, America won't come to the aid of South Korea. To the United States, the islands may seem so trivial that South Korea could give them up for good, and public opinion in America may well favor this attitude.

Wakamatsu: That is a delicate problem. In short, the mission of the American troops in Korea is to cope with any aggressive acts by North Korea against the south. Should South Korea invade the north, therefore, they would not be bound to join her in her march northward.

Fukuda: Just as the United States has her bases in Japan to keep the country from arming, so it is possible that her troops are stationed in South Korea to keep the country from marching north. Probably because of this consideration, the American troops have not moved down to Pusan, but have decided to stay where they are.

Wakamatsu: So they have. They remain in Korea to keep watch on her, too. It's a delicate problem how they would react if South Korean forces crossed the 38th Parallel.

Passin: The reaction may depend upon the situation in which the incident took place. It's hard to imagine the U.S. supporting South Korea if South Korea made the first move. But I cannot imagine that South Korea would act that way.

Muramatsu: As things stand today, we fear the western islands may not be defensible. North Korea's 202mm guns can hit the islands. Although South Korea may be inclined to escalate the war under the circumstances, her armed forces, except the garrison in Seoul, are under the command of the United States forces in Korea. Therefore, she cannot attack without the approval of the American Commander-in-Chief.

Wakamatsu: Anyway, the western islands cannot be ignored or slighted. Sometime in 1975 or other, North Korean planes flew over the islands many times and South Korea was on the alert. If we think over this matter, we can easily see that the islands are vulnerable to physical as well as legal attack by North Korea when the United Nations forces are gone.

Muramatsu: If and when the islands are taken, North Korean planes can skim over the surface of the seas and make a surprise attack on Seoul.

Wakamatsu: Obviously, the islands have radar fences and this gives a strategic value to them. If they fall, South Korea's defense will suffer as if losing an eye.

Seoul is militarily vulnerable because of its proximity to

the Military Demarcation Line— a distance of only 40 to 50 Km—and to the seacoast. Geographically, South Korea is at a disadvantage since the north could make use of the Ongjin peninsula and other coastal lines for covert operations against the south.

Moreover, the terrain north of Seoul doesn't provide any natural defense line. If North Korean troops cross the Imjin River, the boundary between the two halves of Korea, they encounter no barriers down to Seoul. Once the city with its millions of population comes under the attack, a panic will certainly follow.

What if South Korea is communized?

Kase: To change the subject, what impact would the communization of the Korean Peninsula—although this possibility is slim at present—have on Japan? Professor Reischauer says Japan won't be affected by that and some Japanese scholars of international politics concur with him. I wonder whether this argument is indisputable.

At present, Hokkaido is the only place in Japan where a threat from the Asian continent is felt. Therefore, the Japanese Self Defense Forces deploy one-third of the 150,000-man land force in Hokkaido. More than half of its 700 tanks are there. Also, more than half of its artillery and about 90 percent of its heavy guns are concentrated in the area.

To sum up, top priority is given to the northern territory while Kyushu in the south is almost completely undefended. If the whole Korean Peninsula is communized, Japan will have to defend not only Hokkaido but also Kyushu. How will the Japanese be affected psychologically then?

Fukuda: For one thing, there is a sense of security that everything will be all right as long as America is with Japan. Some people feel assured that Americans will protect them even if the whole of Korea comes under the thumb of the

Communists and Japan is isolated in Northeast Asia.

On the other hand, a view à la Mr. Yamamoto Hichihei on the Japanese race is prevalent these days that Japan is a nation that, even if communized, can make it by hook or by crook.

Wakamatsu: Some even think it would be better for Japan to be communized.

Fukuda: Of course, they do. They oppose communism but will accept it if circumstances dictate. Surprisingly a large number of Japanese share this view. In South Korea, almost all people stand against communism. But it seems that to the United States, Japan, not South Korea, is more congenial.

We have discussed the Japanese-American as well as the Japanese-Korean relations, but the problem is really the Korean-Japanese relationship. What sort of relationship do we see between Japan and South Korea? Mr. Muramatsu said ambivalence exists between America and Japan. I think this also applies to Japan-Korea relations. A feeling is prevalent in Korea that they welcome Japan's economic cooperation, but not her military support.

Wakamatsu: This feeling is very keenly felt today.

Muramatsu: The Japanese generally hate Koreans, be they North Koreans or South Koreans, though this attitude has been changing markedly in recent years.

Fukuda: A survey conducted last year by the Cabinet Research Office reveals the countries most disliked by Japanese are North Korea and South Korea while that most liked is America.

Muramatsu: Not the Soviet Union most disliked?

Fukuda: The Soviet Union and Korea have vied for first place, but recently · · ·

Muramatsu: Isn't Soviet Russia overwhelmingly disliked

68

these days? (*Laughter.*) Although no Japanese admit it openly, some people seem to prefer a divided Korea. As the South Korean economy makes great strides, Japan is beginning to regard her as a rival, and is a little bit worried about the emerging country.

Fukuda: Conversely, Koreans have the same ill feeling toward the Japanese.

Wakamatsu: The feeling is stronger on the part of Korean people. When surveys are conducted on the attitudes of Korean people, Japan tops the list in most cases as the country least liked.

Dr. Rhee Syngman allegedly said in the midst of the desperate battle during the Korean War: "However hard pressed we may be by the North Koreans, I would rather join them and fight the Japanese troops, should the Japanese be sent to our aid." The feeling against Japan may not be so strong today, but it hasn't been eliminated completely.

Even if Japan were not constrained by the constitution, she would find it hard to cross the sea and come to the aid of South Korea in case something went wrong there. That might rub her in the wrong way. In the worst case. the south and the north might join hands and jointly confront the Japanese.

Fukuda: Then comes a Japanese-Korean war.(*Laughter.*)

Wakamatsu: So it's impossible to help her militarily. What we can do best would be to permit America to freely use her bases in Japan.

Kase: Then economic cooperation !

Wakamatsu: Yes. But, here, too, we should first understand Korea's situation. We shouldn't be too profit-minded. The principle of live-and-let-live should be honored. Otherwise, we will only be incurring further rancor.

America's current irresponsibility

Fukuda: The Japanese media are largely responsible for making Korea the first or second most hated country. Mr. Passin has referred to this point. The Japanese media are influencing their American counterparts or else the reverse is the case.

Passin: Almost all American correspondents in Japan read only the English language newspapers here. But it is also true. I think, that the Japanese press has been influenced very much by the elite U.S. press, say the *New York Times* and the *Washington Post*.

Fukuda: Perhaps that's true. The *Washington Post* and the *New York Times* probed the Watergate scandal to the bottom. This may have led the Japanese papers to think they would be disgraced unless they pursued the Lockheed scandal in the way their American counterparts have done. They take the American papers for a model, and justify themselves.

A similar case is the withdrawal of the United States ground troops in Korea. The Japanese tend to be influenced by the way of thinking in America that America no longer needs South Korea or she won't care if the whole Korean Peninsula is communized. The Japanese intellectuals look upon the American Democratic Party as an intellectuals' party and are susceptible to its influence.

Another problem is that South Korea and Japan should not be left where they stand today, but be brought into closer relationship in the days ahead. Then comes the problem of Taiwan. Last year I was surprised to read an article in *Newsweek* magazine that the *Saemaul* (New Community) Movement in Korea and the Cultural Revolution in China were the same. That's a cooked-up story.

Also last year I read another article in the September 6

issue of *Newsweek* under the heading, "The Taiwanese Knot," implying as in the case of the Gordian knot that Taiwan constitutes a political headache. The article said in effect: The stumbling block to America is the American-Chinese Treaty committing the United States to the defense of Taiwan in case of war while the Shanghai Communique describes Taiwan as "part of Communist China." The article raised a question of how this contradiction was to be settled.

I was surprised because the Shanghai Communique states Taiwan is "part of China," not "part of Communist China." I carefully followed the "letters" to the editor column in the succeeding issues of the magazine, and was amazed to find that no reader ever took issue with the term "Communist China." It can be said, therefore, that the general public in America thinks that the Shanghai Communique of 1972 recognized Taiwan as part of Communist China. As I cited one or two examples in my book, *Nichibei ryokokumin ni utsutaeru* (An Appeal to Japanese and American Peoples), the American public thought that way when I visited the United States in 1973.

Wakamatsu: It's a serious misunderstanding.

Fukuda: But I can't simply brush it aside as a misunderstanding because rumors have it that a secret understanding was made in Shanghai. I feel there does exist a secret agreement. I am inclined to think Nixon told Chou En-lai that it is "part of China" outwardly, but in fact is "part of Communist China."

So the Carter Administration will no doubt bring about a closer relationship with China. What will be the future of Taiwan then? Indeed, this is a Japanese-Korean-Taiwanese question.

Kase: Forming a triangle, Japan, Korea and Taiwan are achieving the fastest pace in economic growth and prosperity throughout the world.

It has been possible for the three to do so because America has protected Japan, South Korea and Taiwan. Now her commitment to Taiwan is faltering and there has emerged a new age of American irresponsibility, I think.

Fukuda: At the close of the article in question, in the September 6, 1976 issue of *Newsweek*, Senator Hugh Scott, one of the closest friends of Nixon, gave an account of his trip to Taiwan to a group of Washington newsmen. He said he had warned the Taiwanese that they should not take the "American defense umbrella for granted."

I wonder why they don't say to Japan, "it will be a great mistake if you think Japan will remain forever under the umbrella of the United States." If they were to say so, Japanese-American relations would be rejuvenated. Asian countries are now striving to promote their ties with Japan and other advanced countries. America in turn should make greater efforts to better her relations with Asian countries.

What can be done about mutual distrust between Japan, Korea and America?

Japanese lack common sense in international affairs

Passin: A little while ago, I said the U.S. is in a period of transition. The foreign policy of the earlier, cold-war era is being reviewed and reassessed, and Japan will be running a serious risk not to take part more positively in this review process. At present, Japan provides almost no input. To the extent that information does flow in from Japan, it is taken with a grain of salt.

This is not the problem of the U.S. and South Korea alone. This is also Japan's own problem. Our two countries, or rather Japan, Korea and the U.S., should jointly and actively tackle it. Unless these three countries engage in discussions from now on, things could become very dangerous.

Fukuda: In a sense, the communication line between Japan and America has been to date kept largely through Professor Reischauer.

Muramatsu: Now comes Ambassador Mike Mansfield!

Wakamatsu: The line has become so thin that it's almost non-existent.

Kase: To a great extent, Japan is responsible for that.

She depends on America in a happy-go-lucky way and lacks training in asserting her position vis-a-vis America.

It was the Tanaka Administration that forsook Taiwan in the first place. Although Japan was to vindicate Taiwan, she was the first to desert the country. After all, Japan could do this under the umbrella of the United States. Mansfield proposed in the United States Senate that America adopt the Japanese modality in establishing relationships with China. And Japan has already done that irresponsible act.

When detente was the order of the day, its advocates said if detente were abandoned the cold war might revive. But the truth is that even if detente collapses, the cold war will not revive.

One of the major characteristics of the cold war was that America maintained an enormous network of overseas military bases and defended the free world almost single-handedly. What is detente then? It is in short an expedient that Soviet Russia has used for mastery of the world.

Revival of the cold war would be welcome since it would serve the cause of protecting Japan's security as in the past. Now that America is beginning to retreat to her mainland, we can no longer expect the revival of the cold war. The advent of a new era is in the offing.

Fukuda: I call it cold peace, not cold war. It is a peace imposed on us. Because of the nuclear deterrent, no war can be started even if a country wants to. Therefore peace reigns, a peace that has not been won. We have no choice but to live in peace—a peace that doesn't allow us to make war even if we have a will to do so. This can be called cold peace. This state of affairs will continue well into the future, I believe.

Muramatsu: In this state of cold peace which is expected to prevail in the future, one of the major problems is that Japan is not yet fully prepared to expound her position cogently—though this may partly be due to the present American policy.

Fukuda: But the trouble is that what we have said to Mr. Passin, to the United States or to President Carter may boomerang on us. (*Laughter.*)

Muramatsu: No matter how foolish President Carter may be, we might convince him if we were ready to speak up clearly and logically on a political plane.

Fukuda: If only we were ready to do that!

Muramatsu: It's a miracle that the Socialist Party, having talked utter nonsense for the past thirty years, still holds on to its place as the first opposition party. (*Laughter.*) But Japan still maintains its irrational and absurd position as symbolized by this case of the Socialist Party. Japanese apply a kind of logic that too often baffles foreigners. As long as this mentality persists, we cannot hope to win the confidence of other countries however hard pressed we may be.

Kase: The Japanese journalists should share the responsibility for that. To cite an example, Messrs. Oda Minoru, Miyoshi Tetsu or others like them visit North Korea and have the impudence to say the north is far better off and a paradise for laborers.

Joan Baez, a famous American folk song singer, was once a symbol of the anti-Vietnam war movement. However, since the communization of Vietnam she is leading a protest movement against the atrocities being committed in that country. Ludicrous it may seem, but it is in fact a sad story.

Muramatsu: In other words, she is now admitting what a fool she has been.

Kase: But Mr. Oda Minoru and company are closing their eyes to what is unfolding in South Vietnam now. They may be doing so on purpose, but I think they aren't courageous enough to recognize publicly the realities of Vietnam.

Wakamatsu: As Mr. Passin has already said, South Vietnam, Laos and Cambodia are becoming a hell on earth. Completely disregarding the sober facts, they appear to have just one answer ready—when questioned about the atrocities being committed in these countries—that they have never heard about them or that they are simply groundless rumors. It doesn't make any sense.

Fukuda: They are professional anti-war activists, and are no longer concerned once the war is over.

Muramatsu: Their business ends there.

Fukuda: So they, like vultures, are searching for a place where a war is brewing.

Kase: The case of Mr. Honda Shoichi is worse yet. Tens of thousands of Vietnamese have reportedly died while attempting to flee their country by sea. But Mr. Honda reverses the case by labelling them reactionary elements who tried to escape because they were being forced to adjust themselves to the new order " in freedom."

Fukuda: Maybe Mr. Oda is anxious to see the north invade the south. If a war breaks out, he may start his business anew, leading the van of a pro-North Korea front organization. A cause for joy!

Muramatsu: Or a merchant of death!

North Korea's mobilization capability is the greatest in the world

Kase: It may be presumed that China is opposing the withdrawal of the American troops in Korea.

Wakamatsu: I don't think she is in favor of it either.

Kase: It is said when President Nixon went to Peking, China clung to the United States, out of fear of a Russian attack. If America forsook South Korea, thereby dishonoring the defense treaty between them, China, having no treaty with America, might well become even more worried over how America would respond in case of a Russian attack.

Passin: Another point. If war comes to the Korean Peninsula, the Soviet Union will no doubt provide the north with large amounts of military assistance. That would make it dominant there. China would naturally be concerned about that and would feel that it has to provide aid too in order not to lose footing in North Korea. But in this kind of competition, the Soviet Union is much stroner.

Kase: During the Vietnam war, China and Soviet Russia competed in providing aid to North Vietnam. Soviet Russia being overwhelmingly stronger, the end result is that North Vietnam has come under the influence of Russia. If war breaks out in Korea and the peninsula is unified on the terms of the Communists, it would be the Russian troops, not the North Koreans, who would go down to Pusan.

Passin: That would be another major extension of Soviet military power.

Kase: Then Japan will be facing the Russian troops not only across the Soya Strait and in the northern territory, but in Pusan.

Wakamatsu: To China, who is confronted by Soviet Russia, a war in Korea implies that the whole peninsula might slide into the grasp of the Russians if something goes wrong. Therefore, China doesn't want North Korea to start any trouble.

Once Kim Il Sung started a war, China would not let her go down the drain. And she would inevitably do something to save the north. For the time being, however, China doesn't want any trouble. I cannot predict several decades ahead, but the Sino-Soviet conflict does have some ramifications for the

Korean Peninsula.

Muramatsu: In 1947, then Secretary of State Dean Acheson made a famous speech at the National Press Club. He said the American defense line extended from the Aleutian Islands, to Japan and the Philippines, and excluded South Korea. By then South Korea had secured abundant intelligence reports that the north was going to invade the south, but America ignored them.

Perhaps there had been no Russian tanks on the soil of North Korea by then. But immediately before the war, some 300 T-34 tanks were brought into the north, which enabled the north to launch the invasion. There is no assurance that the Russians will not replay the game. MIG-25's are already there. They cannot be handled without the help of Russians.

Now China. I don't know whether it is true or not, but a story goes that when Kim Il Sung went to Peking immediately before the fall of South Vietnam, Chou En-lai, who was alive then, told him bluntly: "You are free to start a war in Korea, but you won't be welcome in Manchuria when you are forced into retreat."

Wakamatsu: That's probable.

Muramatsu: When Poplar Tree Incident took place in the summer last year, the north axe-murdered two American officers and wounded nine South Korean soldiers.

At that time, the north issued mobilization orders to regulars, the Worker-Peasant Red Guards and the Young Red Gaurds totaling some 3 million. 3 million were mobilized from a population of 16 million. The ratio is unprecedentedly high in world history.

Passin: Except for Israel.

Muramatsu: Even in the case of Israel, the ratio is 360,000 troops out of 3 million or 12 percent of the population. Switzerland has 700,000 troops out of 6 million population or about 12 percent. In the last phase of World War II, Japan had a total of 8 million in the services, or 12 percent of the mainland population of 70 million. So 20 percent is unprecedented in world history.

I remember that during World War II we could see no males in cities because 12 percent of the people had been called up. All the youths and men of early middle age were gone.

Wakamatsu: Production halts, too.

Muramatsu: North Korea mobilized her troops in great strength while America called in B-52's, ordered the aircraft carrier Midway into Korean waters, and raised the readiness level of American troops in Korea to Defense Condition 3.[4]

At that time, the Chinese delegates were conspicuously absent all through the meetings in Panmunjom, as if they were keeping themselves from getting involved in this folly. When we take this episode into consideration, it is possible that Chou En-lai told Kim Il Sung that he would be free to start trouble in Korea but would never be welcome in Manchuria if he were forced into retreat.

Wakamatsu: Also, at that time, the North Korean ambassador in Peking said at a reception that he believed China would certainly come to the aid of North Korea. He had to say so because China had not revealed her intention to back up positively the north on Poplar Tree Incident. China didn't say publicly she wouldn't support North Korea, but she must have looked the other way. She wasn't willing to get involved in such a senseless matter—a situation resembling the hooligans picking a quarrel with the people who were trimming the foliage of a poplar tree and murdering some of them. The Soviet Union, too, must have felt the same way.

4. The lowest level is Defense Condition 5 and Defense Condition 1 means war.

Muramatsu: Wasn't that masterminded by Kim Chong Il?

Wakamatsu: Yes. If such a man replaces Kim Il Sung, who knows what he will do.

Kase: I think North Korea is an Idi Amin Government in Asia, or something like that.

Wakamatsu: It's indeed a strange country.

Muramatsu: But we don't know how China will react if the Soviet Union steps up her military aid to North Korea. Some say the north is getting its MIG-19's from China. A competition in aid similar to that in Indochina may develop between the two countries. That possibility cannot be ignored.

It's Japan's problem after all

Kase: Mr. Carter was only a one-term Governor of Georgia, and has no experience with the Federal Administration. He is quite an amateur in the field of international politics though he has a group of brains beside him and is studying the subject.

I met a Congressman in America, and what he said is very interesting and suggestive: "Postwar America has created three populists—George Wallace, George McGovern and Carter. By nature, a populist isn't fit to be a President, but many factors have combined and militated favorably to make Carter a President." He concluded that a consideration of the United States' world-wide responsibility inhibits a populist from becoming a President.

From now on, Mr. Carter will continue to learn many things. Judging from his initial achievement, however, we are very much worried. In Japan, a Carter boom is in progress and the newspapers are speaking highly of him. But Japan may be the one which will suffer most from his policies.

Fukuda: She is *The Fragile Blossom* ![5]

Passin: At present, Mr. Carter is preoccupied with internal politics, but he is gradually learning many things.

Fukuda: I met Professor Edward G. Seidensticker[6] about a month ago. He said that following the presidential election, the popularity of Mr. Carter would go up among the public, but that there was one place in America where he wasn't so popular. Professor Seidensticker asked where I thought that place was. Since this is a sort of puzzle, like trying to discover the criminal in a mystery novel, usually it is intended to take the respondent or the reader by surprise.(*Laughter.*) I asked if it wasn't the State of Georgia. "No, Washington, D.C.," he corrected. (*Laughter.*) That means the White House. I think people there feel uneasy as they watch Mr. Carter move.

So I wonder how the people near Mr. Carter react as Mr. Passin said. Mr. Carter seems to be acting alone, as Mr. Kase pointed out, ignoring his aides such as Mr. Brzezinski. What are these aides going to do? I mean their pressures and advice.

Passin: I think the White House staff has still not yet been pulled together, and right now Mr. Carter is operating a kind of one-man diplomacy. The Congress has not yet responded to his various programs, but it certainly will start doing so. Also, how much influence the various people around him will have will become clearer.

Fukuda: It's the Japan's problem after all. While Mr. Passin generally concurs with what we have complained about, he can pin his hopes on the future of his fatherland,

5. Dr. Zbigniew Brzezinski likens Japan to a fragile blossom in his book, *The Fragile Blossom: Crisis and Change in Japan* (New York: Harper & Row, 1972).

6. Professor Edward G. Seidensticker is the translator of *Snow Country*, the Nobel prize winning novel by the Japanese writer, Kawabata Yasunari (1968).

America. But can we, Japanese, place the same hopes on our government?

Where should we begin correcting our mistaken notion? From the men in responsible positions in the government? General public? Or the press? Unless spurred on by America or forsaken by her, Japan won't start rethinking about herself.

Muramatsu: It is undeniable that the postwar image of Japan has been notoriously poor, but it also reflects American policies. It derives from America's ambivalent way of thinking as we have already discussed. That is, postwar Japan has lived within the framework of American policy which is opposed to her excessive armament, but supports her armament to a certain extent.

In case Japan decides to take an independent line like Europe, even if the Americans were withdrawn, she may follow in the footsteps of Gaullist France. One of the pillars that supported Gaullist policy was the French self-reliance in military and industrial fields. De Gaulle had failed in other fields and was brought down after 10 years. How surprised America was and how strong her negative response was when France stepped up her industrialization and went nuclear all on her own!

By hindsight, however, the Americans are changing their appraisal of him and are thinking that what he had accomplished was essentially right. America showed such a strong negative response even to her ally, France. However hard Japan may try to assert herself and maintain that she is as independent as any European country, America will not view her in that way. Perhaps America sees West Germany from a similar point of view. West Germany as a defeated nation was permitted to arm herself as a component of NATO forces, but not independently. This feeling America has toward West Germany cannot compare with that she has toward France.

In this sense, we can say if Japan decided at this point

in time that she could do it alone without America, America wouldn't let her do so.

Passin: No. The U.S. would not. France and Japan are quite different cases. Japan is an isolated island country, and her situation is totally different. France is a member of the European Community, surrounded by friendly countries, and it can go its own way without upsetting its allies. But, Japan is an isolated country, and she needs both protection and watching.

Muramatsu: If Japan decides, as European countries do, to depend upon her own defenses—without nuclear armament—America will be vexed. Unfortunately, Japan, unlike European countries, stands alone and cannot confront the colossal Russian war machine on her own. It would require an enormous military capability for Japan to stand against the Soviet Union even for a month. But America won't try to understand this.

Passin: No one in a responsible position in the U.S. is seriously thinking about abandoning Japan. Most American leaders are willing to maintain the U.S.-Japan treaty as long as possible.

At the same time, there are some people who are urging that the U.S. should withdraw from Japan as well as from Korea. But the majority of Americans still favor defending Japan. Again the problem is what course Japan will take.

Fukuda: Aside from you, all of us are Japanese, but we simple cannot predict what course of action Japan will take in the future. (*Laughter*.)

Passin: I'm sorry to hear that! (*Laughter*.) The Japanese don't know what they should think about the defense of their own country. They don't know what to think about Asian problems either. We Americans are always getting mixed signals from Japan. The government says one thing, but the media another. Today the conservatives and progressives are about equal in strength. We naturally wonder whether we can trust what the present government says and what the next government might do. Japan must make its position clear.

Otherwise, the discussion in America will be concluded unilaterally with possibly entirely unexpected results. Right now the majority view favors the defense of Japan, but I am a bit worried whether this attitude will continue for long. The Japanese are taking a terrible risk unless they make a more positive input.

Muramatsu: I agree. It is obvious that if Japan doesn't apply an internationally acceptable logic and solicit or request America to review the defense problem, America will not understand Japan's position. It is surprising to see how the Japanese media tend to equivocate and how Japanese politicians try to shirk the defense problem, as I said before. We have raised this question repeatedly, but failed to achieve the desired result. Now, Mr. Fukuda has given up almost 95 percent of his hope. I also am down by 75 percent.

However, I venture to say that the problem originated from the fact that the United States emerged from World War II as vanquisher and Japan as vanquished. Japan has not only lived within the framework of the American occupational policy, but has been subject to many American policies imposed upon her. She has inured herself to this. But America should now take a new direction to snap Japan out of this habitual inertia.

Kase: In February last year when the Miki Takeo Cabinet was in power, I was told the following story by a Secretary of the Ford Administration: "When Foreign Minister Miyazawa Kiichi came to Washington, D.C. and asked the American Government to reconfirm that the United States has the obligation under the Japanese-American Security Treaty to defend Japan in case of an armed attack, the American Government accepted and reconfirmed it. Then came Prime Minister Miki Takeo who asked for reconfirmation, too. We complied with his request because of the treaty. The American commitment to Japan implies that we, Americans, are ready to defend Japan. So long as we are bound by the treaty, we are ready, and will be ready, to reconfirm this if Japan so requests."

Then the Secretary asked whether the Japanese Government has ever asked its people to recognize that they are duty-bound to defend their own country. I was quite at a loss for an answer.

Wakamatsu: He hit the nail right on the head.

Kase: The Japanese may refute this by saying that the Americans forced Article 9 into the Japanese constitution or that Japan is a special case. But this argument will not hold water any longer. The American side may retort that more than thirty years have passed since the end of the war, but Japan is still giving the same evasive answer. That is no longer valid. Japan is not a special case, but is simply a scheming security freeloader. Moreover, America, too, has special problems to reckon with.

The postwar way of life has come to an end in Japan. The Japanese should clearly perceive this, or the Japanese-American alliance may collapse.

Passin: As you say, Japan has been very self-serving.

Japan overestimated

Kase: Japan's case is a special one, and different from that of other countries, not because she is a peace-loving country, but because of her cunning in trying to maintain her privileged position.

Wakamatsu: I think so. Our mode of thinking toward

the constitution is a little strange, I think. The Japanese people seem to think unconditionally that the constitution, once enacted, should never be amended under any circumstances.

Kase: That reminds me of an interesting episode. When the constitution was promulgated, the *Asahi Shinbun* editorially said "the constitution has an eternal life" and the nation "should be prudent but be ever aware of the possibility of amendment of the constitution." This means that at that time there were still people in their right mind.

Wakamatsu: China has amended her constitution and so has the Soviet Union. The thirty years of the postwar era can be compared to some hundred years in the past when we consider the changes in values and the development of technology in Japan and elsewhere. In this period of upheavals and great change, it is too unrealistic to insist that the constitution should never be amended and that those who advocate its amendment are imperialistic traitors plotting a war. The hard-headed can never catch up with the change and progress going on in the world.

Muramatsu: Japan has historically boasted of the long life of its legal codes. The Taiho Code of 701 had perhaps been in effect for about 1,200 years. (*Laughter.*)

Wakamatsu: The 1,200 years in that age is roughly comparable to 30 years now.

Fukuda: It is because all countries are now open to each other internationally. To come back to the subject of Japanese-American relations, it is pitiful to admit, as all of us have, that Japan won't move unless America takes some initiative first. We have no other explanation but that everything derives from this. Even the leftists we mentioned can be leftists only because they have a feeling of security living as they do under the American umbrella.

I have said it again and again that, because Japan is in this pitiful condition, America should declare to Japan, as she has done to South Korea, that she will withdraw her troops from Japan in ten years and that she is seriously considering it. Then the Japanese will surely begin rethinking their position.

Kase: I have a better idea. Let America enact the same constitution as that of Japan and declare armed neutrality. Then Japan will hasten to arm herself. (*Laughter*.)

Muramatsu: Japan may arm herself, and another world war will break out. (*Laughter*.)

Fukuda: It's opportune now. Ask America while Mr. Carter brandishes his moral diplomacy to give up her policy based upon military power and to adopt the absolutely moral Japanese-style constitution. (*Laughter*.)

Passin: That would be a new kind of cultural exchange.

Kase: Actually I think it is rather healthy that there is a mutual distrust between Japan and America. When we have transcended this distrust, there will have emerged a genuine Japanese-American relationship. Several years from now will be an important period.

Muramatsu: It is true that this lack of trust exists. But how about the general public?

Fukuda: They don't have any. But they will feel a little uneasy about any plan of withdrawing American troops from Japan.

Wakamatsu: Perhaps the strongest opposition to the withdrawal might come from the leftists.

Fukuda: That may be so. Then it will become much more important to acquaint the Japanese people with the grisly facts about their country. Hopefully a mature reflection concerning the real facts of the past will eventually bring

Japanese distrust of the United States to the surface—a country that has continuously distrusted Japan. Only when this mutual distrust is clearly identified, can the two countries move ahead toward building a genuine partnership transcending this barrier.

Muramatsu: Mr. Kase said that a populist from the rural State of Georgia has become an American President. I am sorry to say this in the presence of Mr. Passin, but I think this fact brings to the surface some essential qualities of the United States—moralistic as well as isolationist qualities inherent in America. Now we clearly see the gap that exists between America's responsibility for the world as the leading superpower of the free world and her political temperament.

By nature, the Japanese are more isolationist than the Americans. Essentially, America is a country that immigrants have built, and is naturally international in character. Politically, she may have taken an isolationist policy since the announcement of the Monroe Doctrine, but, essentially, she is international. In the case of Japan, she has fought full-scale wars only twice from the eighth century to the Sino-Japanese war in 1894.

The Mongolian invasion of Japan in 1274 and Toyotomi Hideyoshi's incursions on Korea in 1591 and 1597 were more like skirmishes, not full-scale wars. For the past 1,200 years, the Japanese have lived within the boundary of their islands and come to entertain the belief that they can live in peace unless other countries intervene. It's impossible to imagine that this deeply ingrained disposition will change in a century or so. Often this is misunderstood by other countries. She is overrated either as totally good or bad. It's true that during the 50-year period from 1894 to 1945, Japan did fight many wars. The history of this half-century has made such a deep impression on foreigners that today they regard the Japanese as a bellicose nation bent on forcing her way into the international community.

In fact, the Japanese are a very isolationist people. Since the end of the Second World War, that isolationist nation has, under the pressure of the United States, given up moving outward and has turned inward, becoming even more isolationist. The entire Japanese have become so accustomed to this way of living that they now have a feeling of security in it. Because Japan is very short of natural resources and depends on foreign trade for survival, she cannot help becoming involved in internationalistic policies. But basically she is an isolationist country. America is essentially an internationalistic nation, but, politically has been able to assume an isolationist stance. The reverse is the case with Japan.

In the postwar period, Japan has actively engaged in foreign trade, but psychologically, she still remains in the Edo era (the period of the Tokugawa Shogunate, 1603–1867).

Kase: Let me put it this way. By 1868 the independence of Japan had been imperiled and Japan reacted to this by finding her way into the outside world. In the end, however, she ran wild and started the Pacific War. Again today, she finds her independence endangered. But the Japanese won't allow themselves to go wild again. A time has come for them to deal seriously with the outside world.

Well, when Japan plunged into the Pacific War, she ranked among the three major sea powers of the world, but, in terms of economic power and technology, she was a small power even far below the level of Italy. That small country pretended to be a great power. That was the cause of trouble. On the contrary, today, Japan has become a great power, but pretends to be a small one. This is indeed embarrassing.

What America wants Japan to do

Passin: As for the U.S., my own view is slightly different. To be sure, America is a country of immigrants, as Mr. Muramatsu said, but it has only been since the end of the

Second World War that it became really internationalist. Before that, the U.S. had been an isolationist country. It could afford to be isolationist because it had an enormous land area and it was relatively self-sufficient economically. Therefore it gave top priority to internal problems.

There are still many arguments concerning the origin of the Pacific War. Some argue that President Roosevelt maneuvered Japan into the war while others think Japan started it. But at any rate, the U.S. became internationalist after the outbreak of the war.

American isolationism is deeply rooted, and the U.S. tends to return to it at every opportunity. In that respect, the U.S. does resemble Japan. The fact that it has not become isolationist now is probably because the pendulum has already swung too far away from isolationism.

This situation should be considered an asset to the free world. The positive aspects of the U.S. should be put to good use. Otherwise, the U.S. will, I am afraid, begin to go back to its basically isolationist character. After what has happened in the aftermath of Vietnam, this possibility cannot be excluded. Therefore all of us together should think about how best we can bring support for the U.S.'s internationalist side.

Fukuda: Mr. Passin said that it was after the outbreak of the Second World War that she became internationalistic. I think this is true in terms of her policies. But, ethnically, the descendants of the British people who fled their country form the nucleus of the American community. They have built a new nation, and people from other European countries have followed in their footsteps. So it is a country built by people who had an inclination to go beyond their national boundaries. As Mr. Muramatsu said, therefore, they have an internationalistic penchant.

America is different from homogeneous Japan in that many heterogeneous races have mingled to make a country.

Then it can be said that she is far more internationalistic than Japan, perhaps beyond comparison.

Passin: Because she is internationalistic, it is possible for the U.S. to respond to what is happening in the world, whether for good or for bad. In the U.S., what we call the WASPs have by now become a minority.

American Blacks account for about 11-12 percent of the population and the percentage of Latin Americans is slightly lower. A very large number of Americans have no historical connection with Europe at all. And their political weight is often greater than their numbers. When we think about isolationism in the U.S. today, we cannot ignore the racial issue. Since the people from non-European countries are highly concentrated in the large cities, their political leverage is greater than their share in the total population.

In short, the international character of the population has become less pronounced. If you take a look at a political map of the U.S. today, this is immediately evident.

Muramatsu: You're right. If one lives in a rural town in America, one finds it painful to read only the newspapers that totally ignore the outside world and give an impression that the town is the only human community that exists on this planet. An American newspaper is a sort of circular notice. However, the Japanese papers do report the events throughout the world even if they are often one-sided. From this we can say the Japanese papers are much more internationalistic.

But my view is a little different on the crux of the problem. You say the Anglo-Americans have decreased in number. But they are the descendants of the Vikings and are very active internationally. Although it is said that Latin Americans are less active externally, the Japanese cannot be compared with the Europeans on this point. Few Japanese residents abroad plan to live all their lives in a foreign land.

They work abroad and invariably come back home to spend their remaining years in Japan.

The mentality of the Japanese is well expressed in a poem written around the end of the Tokugawa Shogunate (circa 1867). A stanza of the poem reads: "I leave my *Kyokan* (native place) to seek my fortune abroad. I shall never return home unless the aim I seek has been attained."

The poet's *Kyokan* is located somewhere between Kagoshima and Kumamoto Prefectures. There was a checkpoint at the borderline. Once he crossed boundary, he would never return to his native place unless his goal had been achieved. What were the Americans doing when the poem was in vogue around the close of the Shogunate? They were moving on to the Pacific coast from the Atlantic coast on horseback carrying only blankets with them.

This disposition is shared by Anglo-Americans and Europeans, but not by Japanese. I meant this when I used the expression, "an inbred isolationism." Because of this inbred isolationism, the Japanese had not awakened until Commodore Matthew Galbraith Perry of the United States and his squadron of four "black ships" appeared off Uraga in Japan in 1853 and fired their guns. It is to the shame of the Japanese to have to admit this, but this is symbolic of the isolationist sentiment of the Japanese. (*Laughter.*)

Passin: The Japanese must change that attitude if they are to improve the U.S.-Japan relationship. My point of departure is different from yours, but I think Japan will be in trouble unless the U.S. helps her. The composition of the American population has changed in such a way that the proportion of those groups from whom the internationally active are likely to come has declined. This change in the internal balance of political forces creates difficulties for U.S. foreign policy.

Therefore, the formulation of our foreign policy now requires pressures from Europe and Japan. About 40 percent of the American population is indifferent to either Europe or Japan. To overcome the inertia and the inclination towards isolation that results from this situation, more pressure and input from our European and Japanese allies is needed.

Wakamatsu: You say they are indifferent, and I think Japanese are no less indifferent than Americans. A very few Japanese really care about the withdrawal of American troops from Korea. Most of them simply remain indifferent. Therefore, this is not presented to Japan as a really important issue. Newspapers are writing much about the withdrawal plans, but they do not perceive this as a pressing issue that warrants a serious discussion among the general public. Therefore, even if America presses Japan into doing something, she is not in a position to respond actively.

Passin: I would rather think as a citizen of the world rather than simply as an American. The U.S. is a country of great energy and military strength. You should be thinking of how this energy and strength can be brought to bear on behalf of the world. It cannot be, if the U.S. withdraws from active participation.

The problem, it seems to me, is how to make the U.S. move in the desired direction. But we should not think only in terms of its military strength. The military power of a country does not exist in the abstract, it is related closely to the outlook of the people. The Vietnam war is a case in point. However powerful the American land, sea and air forces may be, the U.S. can do nothing if the people do not have the will to fight. I suggest that you think along these lines and try to figure out how the U.S.'s capabilities can be utilized to the fullest extent.

Wakamatsu: From the viewpoint of utilizing America's capabilities, it is really disturbing to see that American troops are being withdrawn from Korea.

Passin: Japan also bears responsibility for that. She has the responsibility to persuade the American people that the withdrawal of the American combat troops from Korea—a subject that we have discussed intensively and far into the night—is also the problem of Japan.

PART II

SOUTH
and
NORTH KOREA
COMPARED

Participants :

KASE HIDEAKI

TAKASE KIYOSHI

TAMAKI MOTOI

YAJIMA KINJI

FUKUDA TSUNEARI

From left: Messrs. Tamaki, Yajima, Takase, Kase, Fukuda

Profiles of the Participants

Mr. Kase Hideaki

Born in 1936; studied at Keio, Yale, and Columbia Univs.; editor of TBS Britannica; adviser to Hudson Institute and commentator on foreign affairs.

Mr. Takase Kiyoshi

Born in 1929; studied at Tokyo and Ikkyo Univs.; taught at Tokyo Univ. and Municipal Technical College; professor at Takazaki College of Economics.

Mr. Tamaki Motoi

Born in 1926; was once a member of the Japanese Communist Party; since 1955, is working for a publishing company and since 1960, has written extensively on Korean affairs.

Mr. Yajima Kinji

Born in 1919; B.A., Tokyo College of Commerce, 1942; taught at Peking Univ. and Tokyo Univ. of Arts & Sciences, 1953; studied in the U.S., 1963; professor at Tokyo Engineering College.

Mr. Fukuda Tsuneari

Born in 1912; B.A. in English, Tokyo Univ., 1936; commentator, playwright; Chairman, Modern Playwrights Association and professor at Kyoto Industrial Univ.

Politics, the economy, and ordinary life in North Korea

How North Korean statistics are to be read

Kase: I think South Korea is reflecting a rather dark image in Japan. The Kim Dae Jung Incident, the trial of Kim Chi Ha, the alleged "Japanese-Korean connection," the influence-buying scandal involving American Congressmen and former KCIA Director Kim Hyong Wook's recent testimony at the hearings conducted by the United States Congress —all these are creating a bad image of South Korea.

On the other hand, it is reported that North Korea is in great economic difficulty; that she is defaulting on payments for imported goods; and that the whole of her embassy staffs in the Scandinavian countries were involved in illicit traffic in narcotics, liquor and cigarettes. But, generally, I feel that North Korea's image is less smudged here in Japan.

Another problem on the Korean question I encounter when I sample public opinion, is that the Japanese who speak ill of the south usually say good things about the north. Conversely, those who denounce the north praise the south. Few people denounce both of them. I think there exists a mental climate that makes it difficult for the Japanese to take an objective attitude. When the south is compared with the north, the former far excels the latter in terms of economic development, the improvement of people's welfare and the latitude of freedom. What do you think? I think the Japanese are not adequately aware of this fundamental difference.

Tamaki: Since the south and the north are engaged in cutthroat confrontation and keen competition against each other, it is hard to say in a few words which side is superior or inferior. But, in my judgment, South Korea has caught up with North Korea and has been drawing away from her economically and politically from the beginning of the 1970's. The Japanese intellectuals are very critical of the apparent lack of freedom in the south because of the Kim Dae Jung Incident and the proclamation of the Presidential Emergency Measures there. Neither do I think she is beyond criticism. But this degree of restrictiveness is not comparable to the tight thought control in the north. Essentially, South Korea is an open society and the people of the country have a strong voice. So the weaknesses in political skill are supplemented by seemingly repressive measures. But now the skill seems to be maturing rapidly and the problem of freedom may improve soon, perhaps sooner than we may expect.

Takase: It's difficult to determine superficially whether it's good or bad. For an economic comparison, I have the figures published in 1974. I think they are rather outdated, but let me quote them anyway. The trade turnover is 1,100 million dollars for the north, and 11,300 million dollars for the south—I think this figure is a little higher than I expected.

The output of steel is 2,500,000 tons in the north and 3,240,000 tons in the south; automobile production is 10,000 against 60,000; textile production is 450 million meters against 820 million meters; the north produces 5,500,000 tons of cement while the south turns out 10 million tons. In the field of chemical fertilizers, the figures stand at 1,560,000 tons and 1,660,000 tons respectively. The oil refining capacity is 44,000 tons against 40,000 tons, and food grain production is 6,600,-000 tons in the north and 8,170,000 tons in the south.

When macro-analysis is applied, the south far exceeds the north in every segment and seems superior to the north. But the comparison of per capita GNP produces different results.

Roughly estimated, North Korea's population is 15 million and that of South Korea is 35 million. If I do simple arithmetic and work out average figures, the per capita outputs of major commodities are far higher in the north. Then the problem is how to compare the figures and which segment is to be stressed. So I am not so much interested in the comparison of mere economic figures of South and North Korea. Both the north and the south have problems in terms of their political systems, and are politically biased. I think these are problems that cannot be discussed only with the figures published.

Fukuda: You are talking about the outputs of major products?

Takase: Yes. If GNP is to be applied, Kim Il Sung casually mentioned, at the ceremonies marking the thirtieth anniversary of the Korean Workers' Party, that the per capita GNP was 1,000 U.S. dollars—though I don't take figures very seriously as I already mentioned. I think it's actually 500 dollars or so, but these were the official figures. How much is it in the south, Mr. Tamaki?

Tamaki: According to the *Military Balance* the per capita GNP in 1976 is 532 dollars in the south and 250 dollars in the north.

Takase: I see.

Kase: In 1972, when Mark Gayn, a Canadian journalist (*The Toronto Star*), was invited to the north, the editor-in-chief of the *Rodong Shinmun*, the North Korea version of *Pravda*, said it was 236 dollars. But 6 or 7 years ago, they published the figure of 300 dollars or so.

Takase: 325 dollars, to be exact.

Kase: Two years ago, it suddenly jumped to 1,000 dollars in their official announcement.

Takase: North Korea is inscrutable and such extravagant figures easily pop up. When these fantastic figures come up, they cannot be correlated to the previously published figures. Granted that they have attained a per capita GNP of 1,000 dollars, we still do not know what mechanism determines prices or how national income is calculated. We know nothing about them.

Kase: How reliable are North Korean statistics? South Korea publishes neat figures, but North Korea publishes figures that suit her convenience and that cannot but be termed "outrageous" by anyone. I don't know how they work out their figures for public announcement.

Takase: That's a problem. Not only in North Korea but in other socialist countries, statistics are tabulated by factories and double counting inevitably results, watering down figures. I am doubtful to what degree these statistics represent the reality of the economy.

Kase: The purpose of publishing figures is different, I think.

Takase: As I said a little while ago, the North Korean economy is a government-managed one and the figures published are politically contrived. I wonder what good it is for the audiences of newspapers, magazines and TV to base our discussions on these figures. But if a person studies economics, he is tempted to take up official statistics and to infer meanings from them.

Yajima: There is a good example in our neighboring country, China. Around the end of 1950, a Pi Mu-chiao, who had been the Director of the Statistical Commission was dismissed. As the Director, he had had to deal with figures and produce statistics somehow or other. When he was replaced by a new Director, what do you think the Chinese said? They declared "statistics should serve the party." (*Laughter.*)

So, as Mr. Takase said, figures are manipulated for political expediency. Be it 325 dollars or 1,000 dollars, the figures are meant to suit a policy goal. I want to point out that this is common to all socialist countries.

Tamaki: In the case of North Korea, the segments for which figures are omitted are more meaningful. For example, North Korea announces the growth rate of gross industrial output each year. In the 1960's when her Seven-Year Development Plan had had to be extended to ten years until the goals were achieved, the rate was not made public in 1966 and 1969. I calculated back to these rates from the overall figures published after the Seven-Year Plan was completed. Then I found that the rates in these two years must have been recessive, under zero.

Otherwise, I couldn't make both ends meet. In other words, the production was lower than in the previous year.

In the 1970's—to be specific, in 1971 and 1972—the first and second years of the Six-Year Development Plan, no announcement was made. Later the average annual growth rate of 17 percent was published for the 1971–1973 period. The figure for 1973 was 19 percent. When this is subtracted, the average for 1971 and 1972 becomes 16 percent. In the meantime, an overall recalculation was made unexpectedly around the close of the Fiscal Year 1971 (1972). This strange action deprived the North Korean financial statistics of any consistency. As a result, they could not make both ends meet for their 1971 and 1972 statistics and had to adjust their figures all over again. Figures of this kind we cannot trust.

To date, I have warned we should regard this fact not simply as a tangle in figure-work, but as a reflection of grave deficiencies and confusion in the North Korean economy. This is particularly true when I take into consideration the recessive growth rates that twice occurred in the north in the 1960's.

Yajima: One week ago, I attended a discussion group. One of the participants there said South Korea's statistics are in a sorry state. But I think it's his brain that is in a sorry state. If a country is to survive as a member of the community of free nations and to maintain close relationship with market economies in other free nations, she can never publish any irresponsible statistics. Only a very small margin of political bias is tolerated in a free society. I can clearly say this is true so far as statistics are concerned.

A difference between a market economy and a command economy

Fukuda: Why is it? In Japan there are some people who think South Korea is a despotic country. So they may think the south, as does the north, publish only the figures that suit her convenience. But South Korea cannot do that. Why?

Yajima: She could deceive others once, but certainly not twice, both internally and externally. As South Korea maintains a market economy, she has many joint ventures with Japan and trades with America, European and Middle East countries. If foreign countries began to discredit her statistics, she would suffer greatly. She could take in her trading partners once and manage to make short-term profits, but would doubtless lose much more over a long period of time. Even Japan adjusts her figures a little, but tolerance limits for a free liberal country are extremely restricted.

Fukuda: In Japan some enterprises use double account books to cheat tax officers. (*Laughter.*) Maybe that's the limit tolerated in a free society.

Yajima: Tolerance limits are very restricted. If a country adjusts her statistics beyond these limits, she will be judged unsuited for economic transactions in the community of free nations.

Tamaki: Also, in the case of South Korea, statistics are prepared for publishing systematically by international standards. Therefore, most tricks can be exposed by experts.

Fukuda: Can't we say that North Korea should also be mindful of her trade partners' judgment? She cannot pay back her debts and her requests for credits are turned down. On the verge of bankruptcy, she could not get off successfully with any bogus figures. I can say for sure skulduggery won't work after all.

Yajima: Socialist countries have two sets of statistics: One for domestic consumption and another for overseas consumption. They place their emphasis on the former. Some may argue that such figures for overseas purposes will invite troubles. But most socialist countries have no scruples against breaking or ignoring international agreements. So they feel no qualms about tinkering with their statistics. Their way of thinking is basically different from that of the people in a free society.

Now, there is the question of the North Korea's failure to pay her accumulated debts. She has run into staggering amounts of debt to Japan. Japan asked her to send in her detailed economic data so that Japan could study them and decide on deferment of payment, but North Korea simply ignored the request.

Fukuda: People think the Communist bloc can hoodwink us, but there are limits to that.

Tamaki: Since 1966, North Korea has not published any systematic statistics.

Takase: Wasn't that since 1964?

Tamaki: No, partial announcements had continued until

1966. In other words, the Central Statistics Commission had published some overall figures up to that year, but everything came to an end thereafter. Since then, not the Commission, but the Supreme People's Assembly or the likes have aired figures that they consider politically expedient. When these figures are announced, the greatest possible care is taken to make them appear not to be related to the figures of the previous year or the target figures. So the data are in complete confusion.

Yajima: Are the data in disorder? We can infer the economy to be in disorder judging by who says what and on what occasion.

Takase: As Mr. Yajima said, not only North Korea, but all the socialist countries manipulate their statistics considerably to fit the policy goals of the central parties. And the statistics don't reflect the reality of their economies. The statistics of socialist countries are based on constant prices. That is, the prices are fixed at certain levels for, say, 50 or 57 years. The price index of a capitalist country changes every year, but the prices of a socialist country are fixed. So the statistics do not reflect the real picture of her economy.

As I mentioned briefly before, another problem is that the statistics are tabulated by factories. For example, a garment manufacturing factory files a report on its output of garments; a cloth manufacturing factory reports on its production of cloths. The end results will be double counting and inflated outputs.

Tamaki: It won't be too much to say that they can divide factories if they are willing to increase their outputs.

Takase: Yes, that's the problem. Another point that is categorically opposed to a capitalist country is how a socialist country treats service industry in her statistics, which doesn't fit well into a planned economy. She may regard the service industry to be productive, but she uses the term "gross agricultural-industrial output." That is the concept that differs from the "national income" used by a capitalist country. This also is a problem.

In short, there is a significant difference between a market economy model and a command economy model. The latter inevitably tends to be influenced by politics. I think we should consider the political system of a country when we appraise the statistics related to her economic operation.

Tamaki: But the Soviet Union and Eastern European countries release statistics by a Central Statistics Commission, and we can do some guess work. Such statistics do not exist in China and North Korea.

Kase: Even in the case of the Soviet Union, it's hard to know how much she spends on her defense. The United States CIA publishes its estimates, but the margins are great and figures are often corrected.

I'd like to ask Mr. Yajima. What are the purposes of North Korea and China in publishing their statistics? Do the people engaged in a planned economy really use them?

Yajima: They do, and very craftily. Let's imagine a 10,000 ton work norm is given. Workers strive to meet the norm in one way or another. To take corrugated cardboards, for example, they produce ones that well up in bubbles. (*Laughter.*) Anyway the weight becomes 10,000 tons. No consideration is given to quality. So average workers take advantage of the figures. They try to create the maximum effect with the minimum work. Functionaries in higher echelons use these output figures for political purposes.

Tamaki: In other words, the Soviet-style centralized planned economy is solely after quantity, and ordinary workers endeavor to reach norms only without considering quality.

In North Korea, fishing workers are said to be so obsessed with their norms that they catch only jellyfish that is watery.

Fukuda: Not only figures, but products are watered down. Or should I say they are soaked in water? (*Laughter.*)

Yajima: So quality control becomes one of the most pressing questions in socialist countries. Their leaders stress again and again throughout the year that quality should be thoroughly controlled. This means the improvement of quality has been well-nigh impossible due to the inherent short-comings in the mechanism of socialist economy. The general public is also well aware of this and is taking full advantage of these shortcomings. If the economy is said to have taken a turn for the better, it's due to accidental factors, not to the merits of the mechanism. To shake themselves free from the "economy of poverty" is their slogan. But, ironically enough, they are experiencing a vicious circle of the "economy of poverty."

Takase: Mr. Kase mentioned the defense budget. North Korea's expenditures for defense take up 16.7 percent of the national budget this year. But the defense spending should include not only direct military expenditures, but indirect spending for many related segments. For example, an iron and steel plant can be considered either as a defense industry or a peace-time industry. By the same token, a truck can either become a combat vehicle or a means of transit for the general public. This must be taken into account when we discuss the military budget of a socialist country and we should be able to discern the underlying motives behind their political stance. If we see only the economy, we will not be able to grasp the actuality of that country. When they say they produce one million tons of steel, we should see for what purpose that much steel is being produced. This question can be posed for South Korea, too.

Let us take for example the Pohang Iron and Steel Company. Some Japanese may think it is a defense factory while others may argue it's a peace-time industry. The products from this sort of factory can be used for either purpose. It's difficult to say to what extent a factory is military or peace-oriented in nature. Therefore, our judgment should be based not on individual factories, but on the fundamental policy of a country. Therefore, we should determine what the basic policy of North Korea or of South Korea actually is.

Yajima: They are not limited to raw materials and iron and steel. The cars that Japan is exporting in large numbers could become weapons, depending upon who uses them. Worse yet, instant "cupnoodle" could provide an ideal meal for soldiers in the trench. So we cannot say that Japan isn't exporting weapons. We think we don't, and we don't really care who will use what we export.

Fukuda: Cloth can be used for military uniforms.

Yajima: In a sense, therefore, Japan is a major exporter of weapons. For example, we are exporting a large quantity of diving suits to North Korea. The North Korean guerrillas invariably use Japanese-made diving suits at those points on the Han River where the range of the tide is great; seven to eight meters between the highest and the lowest tides. The Japanese export aqualungs, light-heartedly thinking they may be used for skin diving, but the North Koreans have other uses for them. They are used by guerrillas. So it's not only iron and steel that matter.

But I agree with Mr. Takase on the point that the policy goals of a country provide an important yardstick for our judgment.

Tamaki: North Korea is gearing her armament along the lines of a four point military policy. They are 1) arming of the entire people, 2) fortification of the entire country, 3) conversion of the entire armed forces into elite cadres, and 4) modernization of arms and equipment. Of these, most of the expenditures for Points Three and Four are not included in the military budget. Particularly the fortification of the entire country poses a great problem. To build major facilities, factories and storage facilities underground or half-underground becomes a great economic burden.

The difference between southern and northern national goals

Kase: Now, we come to the basic problem: What are the goals of North Korea as a state?

Tamaki: The national goals of North Korea were predetermined even before she became a country. Under occupation by the Russian troops, the North Korean Communist Party (antecedent of the Korean Workers' Party) decided on its basic goals—to build a base for revolution. North Korea exists as a base for carrying out her revolution throughout the whole Korean Peninsula. South Korea—North Korea refers to it as the southern half of the Democratic People's Republic of Korea—is to be liberated and unified through revolution. For that purpose, the northern half functions and exists as a base. This is her basic goal as a state.

Takase: I concur with your view because Article 1 of the North Korean constitution stipulates: "The Democratic People's Republic of Korea shall be an independent socialist state that represents the interest of the whole Korean people" and sets forth its national objective. Article 4 clarifies the guideline that the "ideology of *juche* (self-reliance) of the Korean Workers' Party shall be the guiding principle for activities of the state." Article 10, if my memory is correct, declares that the country will abide by Marxist-Leninist principles.

So I think they are building their nation along these lines. As Mr. Tamaki said, their basic strategy which is founded on the *juche* ideology is to build up the three revolutionary forces: to establish an economic base in the north for liberation of the south, to foster the revolutionary force in the south, and to cultivate an international revolutionary force by winning the active support of the socialist and Third World countries. I think North Korea is pushing toward the construction of a socialist country and unification policy on the bedrock of this basic strategy.

Fukuda: What will happen when unification is achieved? Is that the goal in itself?

Takase: No, the problem is whether they achieve unification or not.

Fukuda: Then what's the national goal of the south?

Tamaki: I think the first and foremost goal of the south is to build a nation-state worthy of the term while coping with the threat from the north.

Yajima: To put it tersely, it is to build a liberal democracy based on capitalist economy.

Fukuda: But neither Japan nor America will believe that.

Yajima: They rather wilfully deny that. But South Korea is going about it in earnest.

Fukuda: She is playing the lone hand.

Yajima: Perhaps so.

Takase: I wonder whether the present South Korea really is a Western style liberal democracy. It's a Koreanized democracy, not a Western style one. And North Korea is too unusual to be called a socialist country. Neither the south nor the north may be explained by the already existing conception of liberalism or socialism. I think conditions in the Korean Peninsula are unique.

As you know, the south and the north are basically developing countries. Both of them should cope with the residual problems from the premodern period before they tackle the problem of modernization. To take the example of the north, the development of a backward country should not be confused with the construction of a socialist country. She faces this two-pronged problem.

A country lagging behind may be ill-suited for parliamentarism and tends to become dictatorial to some extent, be it a bureaucracy-centered government or a military government. It's a lesson we have learned from Western history.

Kase: Some rigid discipline will become necessary.

Takase: Therefore, it may be premature to jump to the conclusion that the south is a capitalistic country or the north is a socialistic one—though they may become so in the future. After all, the abscissa—as against the ordinate—called international relations and the stage of development must be taken into consideration.

Americans are apt to view South Korea as a country that has reached the stage of economic take-off, to rank her among the advanced countries of the world, but to conclude that she is acting in a politically undesirable way. In fact, however, South Korea has not reached the take-off stage. She still ranks as a developing country. Unless one views South Korea from this perspective, one cannot really understand or appreciate the position of her leaders.

A free society cannot be built in a day

Kase: Let's return to the subject of three revolutionary forces. I think the national goal of the north is to liberate the south.

Takase: Yes.

Fukuda: What is the position of the south?

Takase: I think the south also is inclined to do the same vis-a-vis the north. Because the country is divided along the 38th Parallel and is in quite a unique situation, Koreans think differently, much differently from the way Japanese think.

Kase: But I don't think the south intends to attack and thus liberate the north even if it feels threatened by the north. Kim Il Sung must be grossly misinformed if he feels any threat from the south and thinks it will march northward.

Tamaki: I think a little differently about the north. It was in 1972 when the dialogue between the two began that the north really began to feel the threat from the south. It wasn't a military threat. But the north found that the south had begun to make strides economically and socially, and had in this way become a threat.

More importantly, North Koreans would find themselves in a quandary if they found it impossible to liberate the south and thus fulfill their national goal.

Fukuda: They will become vexed if it becomes hard for them to liberate the south.

Kase: Yes, they will. They are afraid that the economic gap between the south and the north will widen, and that in another 5 to 10 years the south will be far stronger in terms of the welfare and living standard of the people while the north will become steadily and increasingly impoverished. These prospects irritate the north greatly.

Tamaki: In fact the north is terrified by such prospects. The north's disruption of the South-North dialogue in 1972 and its fierce attacks on the Park Government all derive from this.

Yajima: The Red Cross conference in 1972 was meant to open up a meaningful dialogue, but it has had an opposite effect. North Koreans saw for themselves the economic development that had already occurred in the south while in the north helter-skelter economic policies had resulted even in their having to default on the payment of their debts.

That conference gave a lesson to the north: It was that military power alone won't be successful and that liberation can become feasible only when the north has achieved superiority in total power.

Kase: The north must have long believed that a climate favorable to revolution would be created in the south.

Takase: Probably so.

Yajima: After Korea was liberated from Japan on August 15, 1945, leftists organized a Korean Workers' Party in the south and fomented riots all the year round. The party opposed the trusteeship system proposed for Korea by the Allied Powers and started a mutiny in Cheju Island. No sooner had Korea been liberated than she was placed under a military government of a sort which the Korean people hadn't experience even during the Japanese colonial era. Then the Communist-inspired uprisings occurred in the cities of Yosu and Sunchon.[1] The situation in the south was extremely dangerous.

At that time, channels of contact were kept open between the two parts of Korea. The returnees from China were in both parts of the country. Among these returnees were Kim Koo[2] and other members of the Korean Government-in-exile in Chungking, China. Pak Hon Yong and other leftists went north. So I presume there must have existed some underground communications channels linking the south with the north. I also think that a Communist revolution in the south

1. On Oct. 19, 1948, one battalion of the 14th Brigade of the Republic of Korea Army that was to be sent to Cheju to put down a mutiny there, revolted and took the cities of Yosu and Sunchon. The uprising that was suppressed six days later was masterminded by around 40 Communists who had infiltrated the army.

2. Kim Koo (1876–1949) was one of the most renowned leaders of the Korean independence movement against the Japanese. He was one of the three founding fathers of the Korean Provisional Government in Shanghai, China, but was assassinated by an army officer in 1949.

116

was a distinct possibility during the period just after the end of World War II.

But it may be dangerous hastily to conclude that the existence of that possibility alone accounted for the series of riots that followed Korea's 1945 liberation. I do think the question of freedom was involved. Certainly, America made some great mistakes in her policies affecting Korea—such as the announcement of the Truman Doctrine (March 12, 1947), and of the U.S. defense line which excluded Korea by then Secretary of State Dean Acheson (January 1950) and others.

As another example, the confrontation between two South Korean leaders, Song Chin Wu[3] and Kim Koo, was symbolic of the throes accompanying the search for a viable political system. Song supported the Allied Powers' proposal of a trusteeship. He believed that the Korean people who had been governed by a colonial power might benefit from a trusteeship lasting about five years. That was the period of time considered necessary for training the Koreans politically and developing their ability to govern themselves. But Kim Koo stood vehemently opposed to the American Military Government. It will take 20 years, 30 years or perhaps even longer for such a new nation to achieve complete freedom from others. A totalitarian society can be built in a comparatively short space of time. But it takes a longer time to build a liberal society.

South Korea experienced troubles of various sorts until the end of the 1950's. These were the prices she had to pay for her freedom and liberty. On the other hand, North Korea was able to implement her land reform and other postwar re-habilitation programs relatively quickly. This is because a socialist command economy can be established in a short space of time. We should take heed of these two different

3. Song Chin Wu (1889–1945) was an educator-journalist-politician and a prominent nationalist leader. He was assassinated four months after Korea's liberation in 1945.

approaches. The case of North Korea resembles that of China where things went smoothly after the founding in 1949 until 1955.

Kase: In North Korea even freedom of residence is not allowed. Living quarters are allocated to individual citizens by the government. People cannot settle down in Pyongyang even if they want to because the population of the city is limited. The government can do that in the north.

Neither do North Koreans have freedom in the choice of schools. Young people whose loyalty to the party is proven can enter the much coveted Kim Il Sung University, but it is closed to ordinary youths. People don't have the freedom to choose their own occupations. Those Japanese who praise the north often say the living quarters of workers are located ideally close to their places of work. This isn't ideal at all. The state controls both residence and occupation. A man may wish to work at a certain factory. But he cannot do so if his home is far away from that factory. Reportedly, North Koreans aren't allowed to read novels these days, or to slake their thirst for reading what they want to read.

Tamaki: They have completely eliminated all the publications which tried to escape the ideological control of the state.

Kase: Publications are extremely limited, and so is travel. If a person goes to his neighboring village, he invariably encounters a checkpoint along the way.

When he goes out of his village, he must notify the police, much as we do when we apply for a visa for a travel abroad. When he arrives at another village, he must again report to the nearest police station. Even within the city where one lives he is not allowed to move to far-off sections of the city. It's a society controlled beyond our imagination.

It is controlled by a single ideology and a monolithic system, but the north boasts it's a "genuine socialist country." Some Japanese have written that North Korea is a

118

paradise for workers. Such may be the case in part of the north. But if they say the north as a whole is a model Communist or socialist country, the strongest repercussion will come from the Communist countries themselves.

Yajima: If it is said that North Korea is a model socialist country, China and the Soviet Union will refute this angrily, saying "China is the model," or "No, it's the Soviet Union." North Korea is an over simplified socialist society or a backward socianst system where terror reigns.

Kase: Recently Kim Il Sung designated his son Kim Chong Il as his successor. Is he about 34 years of age? Not even his age is made public, and we don't know much about him.

Takase: Maybe he is 35 or 36.

Kase: In North Korea, Kim Il Sung and his family are referred to as the "revolutionary family inspiring eternal loyalty" and a campaign is being waged under the slogan, "let's pledge our loyalty generation after generation." In view of this, North Korea is the least socialistic country in the socialist camp.

Fukuda: A cult of personality?

Kase: Yes. But this sort of cult exists everywhere. That of Hua Kuo-feng of China, Leonid Brezhnev of the Soviet Union and so on.

Fukuda: And Stalin was.

Kase: The making a superman out of a leader or his deification can be seen in Soviet Russia, China and other places. But the governing by a family and the idolization of that whole family are unique in the contemporary world.

In the official history of North Korea, Kim Il Sung and his family are portrayed in the way the holy family is in Christianity. Kim's great grandfather is alleged to have led the masses in the fighting against the invading *General Sherman* in 1866.[4] I don't know whether this is true or not. The story may have been concocted afterwards. Anyway, most of the important positions in the north are monopolized by Kim Il Sung and his family.

Tamaki: As far as I can determine, Kim Yong Ju, Kim's brother, is Vice Premier; Kim Song Ae, his wife, is Chairwoman of the Korean Women's Union and a member of the Presidium of the Supreme People's Assembly (SPA); Kim Chong Il, his son, is Secretary of the Korean Workers' Party; Pak Song Chol, his brother-in-law, is the Premier and a member of the Central People's Committee (CPC); Ho Tam, another of his brothers-in-law, is the Minister of Foreign Affairs and on the CPC; Yang Hyong Sop, husband of his niece, is the Chairman of State Inspection Committee and on the CPC; and Hwang Chang Yop, his nephew, is a Vice Chairman of SPA. Deputy Chief of State Kang Yang Wuk, who is the unique non-party member in the highest echelons of the power hierarchy, is Kim's maternal uncle. Even after a quick glance at this survey, we cannot but conclude it's a dynasty that rules the north.

Gen. Kim Il Sung returns home by Russian tank

Fukuda: Was there a legendary hero by the name of Kim Il Sung?

Yajima: Yes. But the present Kim Il Sung in the north is a different man.

Fukuda: Isn't he related by blood to the hero?

Yajima: The age is different.

4. The *General Sherman* was an armed American steamer that sailed up the Taedong River in North Korea, but was burnt and sunk in 1866 by the then isolationist Koreans who were resisting all foreign contact.

120

Tamaki: It's probable that the present Kim simply assumed the name of that legendary hero in order to take advantage of his popularity. Early in the 1920's, Gen. Kim Il Sung became a symbol of the heroic resistance against Japan. From this alone we can see that the present Kim is too young to have been that legendary hero. In his official biography, the present Kim is said to have waged partisan warfare in Manchuria in the 1930's and that he once marched ino Korea proper to engage Japanese troops in what has since come to be known as the Pochonbo Incident(June 4, 1937). But it's doubtful that these heroic efforts were the work of the present Kim. On October 14, 1945, a man by the name of Kim Il Sung showed up at a welcoming rally held in the north. We can assume that the Soviet occupational forces there must have permitted the name to be used.

Fukuda: Kim had been in Soviet Russia until he returned home as a Russian soldier.

Tamaki: Yes. He was said to have come to the north in the uniform of the Russian army and with the rank of major.

Yajima: When a North Korean Central Bureau of the Korean Communist Party was first organized, it was headed by Kim Yong Bom, the organizer of the Comintern. Kim Il Sung became the First Secretary; Oh Ki Sop, a member of the domestic Communist group, and Kim Mu Chong, a returnee from China (the Korean faction), became the Second Secretaries.

Tamaki: No, when around the end of August in 1945 the present Kim Il Sung came back home with the Russian troops, he wasn't called by that name. He was called Kim Yong Hwan or Kim Tong Hwan. Riding on the coattails of the Russian troops, he intimidated Korean Communist leaders into organizing the Central Bureau. This was done on October 13. By that time he had already become a real power. His initial position in the bureau was below those of Oh Ki Sop and Kim Yong Bom. But he managed to become the General Secretary at the third enlarged conference of the Executive Committee of the North Korean Central Bureau.

Fukuda: When did he assume the name of the legendary hero?

Tamaki: At the welcome rally held on October 14, 1945.

Yajima: That was the mass meeting held in Pyongyang, but it was at the third enlarged conference of the Executive Committee of the North Korean Central Bureau held on December 18, 1945 that Kim established his position as a real power in the North Korean Communist Party. At the meeting, Kim convinced the participants that there should be created a completely independent organ of the party in the north. He also succeeded in redesignating the party as North Korean Communist Party. He outdid First Secretary Kim Yong Bom in the race for power, and became the General Secretary. It was a critical moment.

Tamaki: Yes, it was. Kim was allowed to assume the name of that national hero in recognition of his ability in organizing perforce the North Korean Central Bureau of the Korean Communist Party.

Kase: But I read in Kim's official biography that he had begun to be called Kim Il Sung during his Manchurian days. He was around 19 years then, and was called Gen. Kim Il Sung.

At the beginning of the present century, a Kim Il Sung was active along both sides of the Korean-Manchurian border, and was already a legend among the Korean people. His name was spelled in different ways in Chinese characters: 金一成, 金一星, or 金日成. It is quite probable that Kim borrowed the name of this legendary nationalist hero sometime after 1945. But he was using a different name when he returned to the

122

north after the war.

Tamaki: No, the names he used when he returned to the north in 1945—Kim Yong Hwan or Kim Tong Hwan—were his aliases. His real name is Kim Song Ju— 金聖柱 (also spelled 金成柱)—and it isn't certain that he was called Kim Il Sung during the Manchurian days. Some strongly reject this.

Yajima: According to the *Tongil Chosun Yon'gam* (One Korea Yearbook) *1965*, Kim was not listed among 18 leaders of the Korean People's Republic organized after World War II by Pak Hon Yong and other members of the reconstructed Korean Communist Party. In the middle of the roster of the 50-man Central People's Committee, there appears a name Kim Il Sung. But, it was spelled 金一成，and apparently nobody objected that it was misspelled.

Fukuda: Then he has three different names.

Kase: He was said to have engaged in anti-Japanese guerrilla warfare in Manchuria, but wasn't a commanding general. He was under the command of the Anti-Manchurian Resistance Corps led by a Chinese named Yang Ching-yu. When the Japanese troops in Manchuria speeded up their mopping-up operations, Kim fled to the Soviet Union. Just as so often happened during the liberation of the Eastern European countries by the Russian troops, some people came home on Russian tanks. Kim was one of them. He returned home by Russian tank in 1945. It is a wonder that such a young man was picked by the Russians for leadership of North Korea. There must have been more senior candidates for the leadership.

Tamaki: Views differ on that point. Korean guerrillas in Manchuria—roughly estimated at 200—crossed the border and escaped to Khabarovsk in Siberia. The Russian Border Garrison which received them was under the control of then Minister of the Interior Beria, a leading figure in the Soviet

Communist Party. The prevailing view among those who have been in the north is that Kim won Beria's confidence.

So Kim was thoroughly trained as a special agent for penetration into the north. Although little is known about the training period, we can put available pieces of information together and infer that he might have received his training at a training organization for foreigners that the Comintern had established prior to its dissolution.

Yajima: I heard that he appeared in the north as major under the command of Lt. Gen. (later Full General) T.F. Shtikov, Commanding General of the Border Garrison in the Maritime Province of Siberia. The latter was under the control of the Soviet Ministry of the Interior. At the meeting of the Communist leaders representing the five northern Korean Provinces—a meeting that began on October 14, 1945 and lasted four days—Kim became the First Secretary, sitting next to the Acting General Secretary Kim Yong Bom.

Kase: When the present Kim Il Sung—either spelled 金日成 or 金聖柱 —was in Manchuria and Siberia, the Korean Communist Party already existed as an illegal underground organization in Japanese-dominated Korea. Then Kim Il Sung appeared on the scene and began to purge the highly political and independent Korean Communists who had fought underground.

Tamaki: Yes, he did. First to be liquidated was Hyon Chun Hyok, an influential Communist leader in Pyongan Province. He was a graduate of the Keijo (Seoul) Imperial University and had taught at a normal school in Taegu. When the Korean Communist Party was organized, he was sent north as its representative. Hyon advocated taking a moderate position along the lines of a nationalistic democratic revolution and was collaborating with the Korean Democratic Party[5] made up of northern Christian, nationalist and community leaders. He was assassinated in broad daylight in a street in Pyongyang.

Then Kim convened a conclave—formally the Conference of the Devoted Representatives of the Five Northwestern Provinces of the Communist Party—and blackmailed the participants into accepting his plan to divide the Korean Communist Party into two parts: southern and northern. Some witnesses who attended the conference and who managed to survive the purges said that when Major Kim Yong Hwan (present Kim Il Sung), wearing a Russian army uniform, proposed the creation of a North Korean Central Bureau, all the delegates rose in noisy protest. As a result, it was decided to ask General Secretary Pak Hon Yong in Seoul for his opinion. In keeping with the principle of one country-one party, the Korean Communist Party had its Central Committee in Seoul and Pak Hon Yong was General Secretary.

Kase: You mean the South Korean Workers' Party?

Tamaki: No. Not the South Korean Workers' Party, but the Korean Communist Party had its unitary organization throughout Korea. So the delegates thought the party was indivisible and sent an emissary to Pak Hon Yong at the party headquarters in Seoul. They decided to wait several days for Pak's reply. In the meantime, Major Kim Yong Hwan seemed to have maneuvered secretly among the representatives from the five provinces. Several days later when the delegates reassembled, they found the conference site surrounded by armed Russian soldiers. Two to three leaders desperately tried to defend the "one country-one party"

5. Originally organized by the Christian, nationalist and other community leaders in North Korea, the party, like the Chondogyo Young Friends Party, has now become an echo of the Communists with no local chapters and mass following.

principle, but in vain. The emissary returned from the south with the words of Pak Hon Yong, a faithful disciple of Marxism-Leninism: "Obey unconditionally whatever is ordered by the Russian soldiers." Thus the North Korean Central Bureau came into being.

Kase: Pak Hon Yong was to become a Vice Premier only to be liquidated later. Mr. Tamaki, won't you tell us about the history of the purges?

Tamaki: To begin with, Hyon Chun Hyok, who was the most influential leader of the domestic Communist group in the north, was killed even before Kim Il Sung made his appearance.

Kase: Was he assassinated by the Russians?

Tamaki: The assassin was said to be a henchman of Kim Il Sung. So we can say the deed was masterminded by the Russians. Next came a large-scale purge of the members of the South Korean Workers' Party headed by Pak Hon Yong and Yi Sung Yop.

These Workers' Party members were central figures in the reconstruction of the Korean Communist Party and also organized the South Korean Workers' Party along the lines of its northern counterpart. They fled north and remained there from 1945 to 1947. During that time they were incorporated into the newly emerged unitary organization of the Korean Workers' Party. Some of them came to occupy important positions when the Democratic People's Republic of Korea was established. Pak Hon Yong came to hold the No. 2 post as Vice Premier and Minister of Foreign Affairs, and Yi Sung Yop and other leaders of the South Korean Workers' Party once wielded great power in the administration and party.

When the Korean War produced its horrors, the leaders of the South Korean Workers' Party were held solely responsible for the defeat and were purged in large numbers.

Kase: On the pretext that they were American agents.

Tamaki: Yes.

Facts about Kim Il Sung-ism—the one and only guiding ideology

Fukuda: Do you know how many people have been liquidated?

Tamaki: Officially announced death sentences totaled about 10, but a staggering number of the members of the group were involved. They had been particularly influential in the cultural and administrative segments of the organization and they were virtually uprooted. The number of those purged must reach into the thousands.

Fukuda: How many people went north from the south during the Korean War?

Tamaki: Members of the South Korean Workers' Party participated in the war as guerrillas and a considerable number of them went north with the retreating North Korean troops. But they totaled 10,000 to 20,000 at best. Most of them were scattered in the southern mountains.

Yajima: Conversely, a legion of North Korean people fled to the south. Land owners and moneyed people who had been subject to oppression in the north escaped to the south during the Korean War. They were 50 to 60 times greater in number than those who went north.

Fukuda: How about the ordinary South Korean people who went north, excluding the guerrillas you just mentioned?

Tamaki: Few of them deserted to the north. National Assemblymen and other celebrities including Pak Yol who recently died—influential people who remained in Seoul— were kidnapped to the north. But few ordinary people went north voluntarily.

Professor Robert A. Scalapino of the University of California said that during the war 3 million refugees fled to the south from the north while far fewer people—possibly 100,000 —went north from the south.[6]

Kase: The same holds true for the Vietnam war. Many North Vietnamese made off to the south, but virtually none went north.

Fukuda: At the Military Demarcation Line, I looked into the north through a telescope. The North Koreans were clad in white. I asked whether the color wasn't too conspicuous.

Yajima: The white clothes were designed to keep them from deserting. They could be shot if they were caught trying to escape.

Fukuda: It's true. That's what I was told.

Kase: If you look north at Panmunjom, you will see a huge bronze statue of Kim Il Sung. It's about 20 meters tall.

Tamaki: I haven't seen it yet.

Fukuda: It's said to be the largest statue in the world.

Kase: Dictators have occasionally had their statues produced while they were alive—a Brezhnev's statue is said to be standing somewhere in Russia—but none of them ever distributed such statues throughout the country as Kim Il Sung has done. Hitler built none during his lifetime. President Amin built one in Kampala, and . . .

Tamaki: Stalin had many statues of himself erected in his latter years.

Kase: Yes. But Kim has by far outdone them all. In front

6. Robert A. Scalapino, "The Two Koreas—Dialogue or Conflict," *The Two Koreas in East Asian Affairs*, ed. William J. Barnds (New York: New York University Press, 1976), pp. 61 - 62.

of the Revolutionary Museum in Pyongyang, there stands a large statue of Kim in overcoat with his right hand outstretched. I saw a picture taken by a NHK photographer who visited there. It is a huge statue.

Fukuda: Isn't it in gold foil?

Kase: Yes. In the picture a NHK commentator was standing beside the statue and it was about 10 times larger than he was. They gold-foiled the entire statue two years ago and it is being lighted up with illuminations.

Fukuda: It's virtually a gilt bronze Buddhist statue. (*Laughter*.)

Takase: Why do they do this?

Kase: I don't know exactly. But the NHK commentator said to a North Korean: " It's a wonderful statue and we know how the North Korean people admire Leader Kim Il Sung by this." Then he went on to ask how many such statues exist throughout the country, and was told there are about 500.

Fukuda: The largest of the " gilt bronze Buddhist statues " stands on the Military Demarcation Line.(*Laughter*.) That's a way of intimidating the south. It would be better placed elsewhere for North Koreans to see.

Takase: It derives from the serve-the-great-ism, the flunkeyism that Kim hates so much.

Fukuda: Yes, a trimming policy, or obsession with self-revelation.

Tamaki: I should add another thing here. They are building not only Kim's own statues, but those of his parents and deceased wife (Kim Chong Suk). It's unique in the world. The Kims are a holy family.

Kase: Usually in a Japanese school the teacher's desk is placed on the platform in front of children's desks. But, from pictures taken in North Korea, I saw that Kim Il Sung's bust stands in lieu of the teacher in every classroom, from primary schools up through the colleges and universities. The teacher? He stands aside as did an erstwhile movie "narrator" during the silent picture days. This is true of North Korean schools in Japan,too. By the side of Kim's bust,there always hangs a revolutionary slogan. In short, the teacher talks about the ideology of Kim Il Sung and so he stands to one side.

Tamaki: Worse yet, in some schools in the north, we see cigarette butts and ashtrays displayed in glass cases in the drawing rooms. These are the cigarettes and ashtrays Kim Il Sung smoked and used during his visit to the schools.

Fukuda: How did you find out that?

Tamaki: People who have been to North Korea told me about it.

Kase: A beautiful book, entitled the *North Korean Revolutionary Museum*, is in circulation in Japan. Conspicuous in the book is the scarcity of Kim Il Sung's pictures taken during his Manchurian days. There are only two pictures. If we look at them carefully, we see they are too obscure to make it discernible whether the man in them is really Kim Il Sung. The rest of the pictures are paintings. The combat scenes of Kim as an anti-Japanese guerrilla are portrayed in paintings.

Another characteristic is that there are many pictures in the book, showing such items as a floor cushion in the glass case. The caption reads that the cushion was used by the "Great Leader Kim Il Sung" when he visited a certain locality for his on-the-spot guidance. At first glance, I thought it was a relic of the 1930's, but the explanation said the event took place in 1968. That means the cushion is a very recent product. Also there are pictures of a raincoat and other such.

Tamaki: Some of the buses in Pyongyang have vacant

seats with flower vases on them even during rush hours. If a visitor asks what happened in the vacant seat, the invariable answer is that the seat was once taken by Leader Kim Il Sung. (*Laughter.*) And the bus runs that way.

Kase: I heard a subway train also has a seat with a flower vase on it. I mean a vacant seat. (*Laughter.*)

Fukuda: It resembles a trick pulled by the magician *Monkey* in a 16th century Chinese classic novel (*Records of a Journey to the West* by Su Ch'eng-en).

Takase: Then what can we make out? In the north they denounce the flunkeyism in their "learning (indoctrination)" classes. I wonder how this sort of folly is received by the people?

Yajima: By the masses?

Takase: Yes. In the so-called "learning" classes, people are taught the ideology of *juche* or criticism of flunkeyism. Books are written about this subject. But the reality differs from what people are taught. For our part, this sounds strange. How is the difference justified?

Fukuda: They may say they have the Great Leader Kim Il Sung and that those who talk big in other countries are the disgraceful victims of flunkeyism.

Takase: I understand what you mean. But when I read carefully the selected works of Kim Il Sung, I find that he quotes less from Marx and Lenin than Mao Tse-tung or Stalin did. Very little is quoted. Too much quotation may be taken for flunkeyism. (*Laughter.*)

Tamaki: Since the beginning of the 1970's, quotations from other than Kim Il Sung-ism have virtually vanished from all the North Korean publications. On the birthday anniversaries of Marx, Lenin or Stalin, the editorial of the *Rodong Shinmun* devotes most of its space to the adoration of Kim Il

Sung.

Yajima: Mr. Takase, I have read the biography of Kim Il Sung. But it's the least interesting of all the biographies I've ever read.

Takase: Even if we set aside the question of whether it's interesting or not, the biography has never been published in a complete form. There is some difference between the editions published in Pyongyang and by Miraisha in Tokyo. When people read them—though I understand what Mr. Fukuda means—don't they notice the contradictions?

Yajima: Yes, they do. The general public is wise enough.

Fukuda: What Mr. Takase thinks reflects an intellectual way of thinking.

Yajima: The masses are always realistic and clever. As Mr. Takase pointed out, the gap certainly exists. But this also is the case with China and every other country.

Let me take an example from Manchuria. When people are ordered to attend a lecture meeting, they carry with them the books they want to read at the meeting. When the speech begins,they open the books at once, but the speaker doesn't mind that. Why? He knows that he isn't saying what he intends to say. He thinks it natural that the audience won't listen to him. The audience too is ready for that. It's the people's way of coping.

Tamaki: I am amazed to learn that China is a relatively vital society. People regard the men in power as if they were living in another world, and they maintain their own cosmos.

Fukuda: In a certain sense, it is true of Japan, too. The press plays the role of the speaker and strongly attacks Tanaka Kakuei. But his constituents in Niigata ignore all this and return him to the Diet. Good or bad, the masses are realistic on that score.

Takase: They are highly intelligent everywhere.

Tamaki: But North Koreans don't have the books to take to a lecture meeting.(*Laughter*.)What they can carry openly are only the works of Kim Il Sung or text books.

North Korea is a Kim's dynasty

Kase: To return to the subject of one family rule, Kim Yong Ju, a brother of Kim Il Sung—a third son born to Kim's parents and the second one died earlier—is a Vice Premier. His brother-in-law, Ho Tam, is another Vice Premier and the Minister of Foreign Affairs. Another brother-in-law, Pak Song Chol, is Premier. The Mayor of Pyongyang is said to be one of Kim's cousins. If Kim's genealogy is diagramed, it comprises an enormous number of his relatives in key positions. A parallel to this sort of one-family rule is hard to find anywhere else.

Tamaki: Mrs. Bandaranaike of Sri Lanka once moved in the same way. So did Mrs. Indira Gandhi of India—now out of power.

Kase: She tried to have her son Sanjay elected, but in vain.

Tamaki: Isn't this tendency prevailing among Asian rulers?

Kase: When we read the official history of North Korea, we see that without Kim's family it doesn't make a history at all. Excluding Kim's family, only 5 to 6 people are mentioned —and more than once or twice—in the *North Korean Revolutionary Museum*. In the two-volume book, the name of Kim Il Sung is mentioned 1,500 to 1,600 times.

Tamaki: In this connection, I should mention the follow-up purges: First the South Korean Workers' Party members were purged. In the next stage from 1956 to 1958, the Yenan faction (returnees from China) and the Moscow faction were liquidated. Among them were such eminent figures as Choe

Chang Ik, Pak Chang Ok and Kim Kwa Bong who were holding the offices of Vice Premier or of President of the Presidium of the Supreme People's Assembly (the Chief of State). Thus Kim's great political rivals disappeared.

Another round of purges was carried out during the period between 1967 and 1968. This time the men in key positions who originally belonged to Kim's own faction were liquidated. They included Pak Kum Chol, Yi Hyo Sun, Ko Hyok and Kim To Man. As a result, an absolute leadership centering around Kim Il Sung, his family and his sycophants was established. The Fifth Congress of the Korean Workers' Party in 1970 marked the watershed.

Kase: It's a dynasty.

Tamaki: A dynasty has already been established.

Fukuda: A medieval age has come back.

Tamaki: But in the 1970's, some peers of Kim Il Sung still held positions in the top leadership: Premier Kim Il, Vice Premier Choe Yong Kun and Defense Minister Choe Hyon. But all of them are now either demoted or dead. No equals of Kim Il Sung exist today.

Kase: The tombs of the former wife of Kim Il Sung, and those of his father and his mother are called mausolcums in the north. In China the term "mausoleum" was reserved only for an emperor, an empress or members of the royal family.

Takase: Then Kim Il Sung's ruling system has changed from one-man rule by Kim to one-family rule.

Fukuda: That sort of system exists in entrepreneurships in capitalist countries. One often finds one-family management enterprises. So North Korea can better be regarded as North Korea, Incorporated.

Takase: There isn't any reason why we cannot view her that way. Not a Japan, Incorporated, but a North Korea Incorporated, when she is so easily taken as a household

134

enterprise.

Tamaki: So things have gone awry. North Korea, Incorporated is practically broke. Her problem is how to deliver herself from this situation. She must turn to foreign countries for help in one way or another. Over the past two or three years, therefore, North Korea has leaned toward the Soviet Union. But, if the influence of the Soviet Union begins to be felt in North Korea, Kim Il Sung and company will get in trouble because that means the possible emergence of another Russian faction in the north.

Kase: Kim Il Sung may find his own position threatened.

Tamaki: Even if the Kim Il Sung dynasty rules, most of the young technocrats have been trained in the Soviet Union. Bureaucrats, soldiers and engineers are sent to Russia for advanced training because they cannot be sent to non-Communist European countries. Therefore, Russian influence is great in every field. If the Russians attach strings to their aid and send in their advisers to the north, a Russian faction may emerge among the administrative, military and economic segments. This will mean a crisis for North Korea. So Kim Il Sung is in a hurry to firmly establish his dynasty now. This may account for his recent effort to designate Kim Chong Il as his official successor.

Fukuda: With her economy on the verge of bankruptcy, something unexpected might happen such as C. Itoh and Company (Ito Chu Shoji) absorbing the Ataka and Company (Ataka Sangyo) to take an example from the Japanese business world.

Yajima: The more the economy develops the more difficult becomes the management of a family enterprise. Information and talents must be gathered or recruited from non-family members. That possibility had led to the absorption of Ataka by C. Itoh.

North Korea's future relationship with the Soviet Union

inevitably involves this question. Moreover, a family rule doesn't assure tranquility. Rivalry and hatred among the members will occasionally be bitter.

Tamaki: Within the family, yes.

Yajima: That's right. And there are already some signs. For example, in 1954 Kim Il Sung had a sort of shotgun wedding with his second wife, Kim Song Ae.

Tamaki: According to another account, after the death of his first wife, Kim ran after one woman after another and raised the fear that his philandering might end up as a political issue. So some influential insiders such as Kim Il and Pak Chong Ae schemed to place Kim Song Ae, a moderate candidate, for Kim's hand as his secretary.

Kase: Kim Chong Il, Kim's successor, is a son by his first wife, Kim Chong Suk.

Yajima: Yes, Kim has another son named Kim Pyong Il by his present wife, Kim Song Ae. Counting forward from the year of marriage in 1956, his age is estimated at about 20. Fearing that a power struggle might develop between him and Kim Chong Il, he may have been sent abroad to study, and may not be in the north now.

In short, to the heir apparent Kim Chong Il, Kim's present wife is his step-mother and his step-brother has grown up to be a possible rival. Now, conditions are ripe for jockeying for power in the court. What will happen in the two decades ahead? That remains to be seen.

Peculiar social structure and a "back-number" system

Kase: I think the Democratic People's Republic of Korea has two outstanding characteristics. One is that one family rules the country. Another is that it's a small country with a population of about 16,000,000. Being such a small country, it is possible for the ruler to effectively and completely control the people. In this sort of country, the people cannot complain even when what they are taught contradicts reality.

Tamaki: To elaborate on the social structure of the north, the most striking thing is the fact that they have built a completely closed society on the basis of such units as factories and communal farms. Factories and farms alike contain living quarters, day nurseries, schools and hospitals in the same layout. No free transit is allowed between them. Only party members and bureaucrats high up in the echelons of power act as horizontal links in the society.

I think the collectivized farms are important. It seems that people born in a locality are not working there. They are scattered all over the country. This is in part the legacy of the Korean War. People from different places are gathered together on the standardized collective farms. Once settled on a farm, they cannot move at will. We have mentioned checkpoints. These are manned by soldiers with fixed bayonets. Free traffic is completely forbidden.

Kase: A pretext given is that of keeping North Koreans safe from South Korean agents.

Tamaki: So it's completely closed. It's a thoroughly controlled, isolated country. Solzhenitsyn wrote a novel, *The Gulag Archipelago*, but in the case of North Korea, the concentration camps are not located in a remote part of the country. The whole country is a concentration camp. So, when the purgees are scattered among farms, factories and mines, they are destined to remain there for the rest of their lives.

Kase: As there are many party members, surveillance will be to the hilt.

Tamaki: Let me talk briefly about the Korean Workers' Party. It's unique in the world. First, it has had no experience at all in successfully carrying out a revolution. It emerged as the party in power from the very beginning. As a result, only the people on the make acceded to the party. And the lust for success and bureaucracy have become deeply rooted in it.

Second, the number of party members as opposed to the entire population is great. Out of a population of 16,000,000, 2 million are party members or one out of every 8 persons. If only adults are reckoned with, the ratio must be one member to every 4 to 5 people. By households, every 2 to 3 households includes at least one party member. Thus it's possible for the party to completely control and supervise the whole populace. Whenever an election is held in the north, they boast that the turnout is 100 percent and that the affirmative vote is 100 percent—there is only one candidate to be voted on. This alone indicates how tightly the party controls the whole population.

As if it were not enough, they have a "five-family system." Households throughout the country are organized into groups of five and a party member is assigned to each group to guide, supervise and indoctrinate in all aspects of daily life. This system reminds us of the "five-family neighborhood unit" of the Edo period in our own history.

Kase: I have interviewed about 50 refugees from North Korea. They naturally spoke ill of the north—that's why they fled to the south.(*Laughter.*)When I asked them if there was at least one thing good about the north, two-thirds replied there isn't anything good about it. The remaining one-third answered: "In the north, there is no freedom. Neither is there a marked difference between the rich and the poor. Of course, party cadres are enjoying luxurious living, but there's no difference among us ordinary people."

Fukuda: It's total poverty for the total populace (*Laughter.*)

Kase: In the south, they have found out that even among the general public, the living standards differ. In the south they have to compete. But competition in the north consists of flattering the party leaders. Except for the competition in flattery, it's more easygoing in the north. Some answered in this fashion.

Yajima: What strata of people fled to the south? Aren't they mostly of the lower strata?

Kase: Among the refugees I interviewed were some field grade officers with the ranks of major or lieutenant colonel, but most of them belonged to the lower class.

Yajima: I think it's not too much to say that the north is a good place for loafers to live.

Kase: That may be so. And here I want to make it clear that the gap is not very great between the rich and the poor in South Korea. According to the data on national incomes published by the World Bank, they are far more evenly distributed in South Korea than in Japan.

Tamaki: It's interesting that there isn't a real gap between the rich and the poor in the north—except for the privileged class, they are all equally poor. Presumably they derive a sense of security or of deliverance from this state of total poverty.

Takase: In the north, the wages are divided into 8 grades. So it's not without difference. China also uses an 8-grade wage scale.

Yajima: Even if the 8-grade wage scale is used, prices differ by localities and this widens the difference.

Fukuda: North Koreans use coupons when they purchase commodities. So the 8-grade wage scale doesn't mean much.

Takase: If a North Korean worker saves money, he cannot spend it as freely as he wants to.

Fukuda: Because the worker cannot spend money, he has to deposit it in the government-run bank. Thus the state treasury eventually draws in all the money it issues.

Kase: Japanese papers emphasize that the north collects no taxes. That's nonsense. Since the state monopolizes everything, there's no need for taxes.

Takase: From the viewpoint of the socialist principle, it's natural not to collect taxes, and it's unnatural to do so. But there are "contributions" paid to the state. In the north, everything is run in the way the Japan's Monopoly Bureau does. The fixing of prices presents a real problem. What mechanism determines prices in a socialist country? As this important point is concealed, the country becomes essentially a concealed country.

Tamaki: In 1974, North Korea announced a measure for complete abolition of taxes and carried on a fulsome propaganda campaign in which it was trumpeted that "North Korea has become the first tax-free country in the world." Apparently conscious of the Soviet Union and China, where taxes are still levied, the North Koreans stressed: "Our country has now come to enjoy a happy life to the degree where we feel envy of no other country." On the other hand, they attributed this to the "benevolent grace of the Revered Premier" Kim Il Sung and pledged to work for him with absolute, unconditional loyalty in order to repay his beneficence. It was used as an instrument of moral edification.

In fact, however, 98 percent of the north's state revenues come from "socialist management revenues"—obtained from the deductions from the factories, offices and farms. As the surplus labor value of the working masses is taken up by the state in this way, the abolition of 2 percent taxes doesn't mean anything economically and won't affect the living of the working masses.

Moreover, it is said that even a socialist country finds it advisable to retain taxes since they function as an ultimate automatic adjuster. Some members of the privileged classes and professions are still able to enjoy substantial personal incomes, and a gap between the rich and the poor develops.

So the Soviet Union and China maintain a mechanism to collect taxes from the upper-class people. When this mechanism is removed, the state becomes the complete determinant of people's life. It's a serious matter.

Kase: Let me ask you a question, Mr. Tamaki. In the north, social origin is classified into 51 class categories and people are treated according to their class status. This is a unique system, which doesn't exist in other socialist countries.

Tamaki: Social origin means social background, and it breaks down into fifty-one class categories.

Kase: Admission to educational and employment opportunities is determined by such criteria.

Tamaki: One-third of the classes are called the "ordinary classes." These include workers and the farmers; small farmers, poor farmers, and middle-class farmers.

This classification overlaps with political classification by which it is determined whether a citizen is a member of the Korean Workers' Party, of the Korean Democratic Party or of the Korean Chondogyo Young Friends Party.[7] It is also determined by whether he was a collaborator with the Japanese colonialists or with the South Koreans during the Korean War, or whether a member or members of his family deserted to the south. In all there are 51 classes.

Fukuda: The whole family is collectively affected by that.

Tamaki: Yes.

Kase: The lives of children and grandchildren are affected by the system.

Yajima: Even one's distant relatives and those of his

7. One of the mass organizations that the north maintains to create the impression that it has a number of non-Communist organizations. The Chondo-gyo. (The Teaching of the Heavenly Way) is one of Korea's traditional, indigenous religions.

wife's distaff or spear side are affected.

Kase: Classification is recorded on the identification cards which must be carried at all times.

Tamaki: The party and the government maintain all these records. Employment, admission to schools and other matters are affected by them and identification cards are checked whenever one travels.

Kase: Classification also determines the places one can live.

Tamaki: Everything is under control. Really the "back-number" system or serial number system for the whole populace that the Japanese progressives so oppose is in full force in North Korea.

Fukuda: It makes us green with envy that they can accomplish such colossal things. (*Laughter*.)

Foreign relations completely deadlocked

Takase: Let's now turn to the subject of North Korea's international relations. In a word, North Korea's diplomatic relations are in a state of deadlock with all countries. Since the Sino-Soviet confrontation isn't so simple, Vice Premier Kong Chin Tae shuttled to Moscow and Peking several times last year alone. North Korea must work out long-term plans and clear herself of foreign debts. Presumably she is seeking economic assistance, but neither the Soviet Union nor China is apt to readily comply with her requests. The north has also come to understand that she won't be seated in the United Nations on the strength of China and the Soviet Union alone. Now, she may think she cannot expect much from these two Communist countries.

Thus her foreign policy has begun to change a little. She has turned to the Third World countries and tried to expand contacts with them. But in August last year the north suffered a setback at the fifth summit meeting of non-aligned nations in Sri Lanka. Fifteen to sixteen years have passed since the Third World countries began to advocate their non-alignment policy and most of them are politically independent today. Their chief concern has shifted from political issues to economic issues. But North Korea is still obsessed with the political problems attendant on the 38th Parallel and gives top priority to political issues. Therefore, her plea failed to strike a sympathetic chord in the Third World.

Is the Soviet Union friendly to North Korea? I don't think so. The Russians may find Kim Il Sung-ism both repugnant and insolent. But they can't act carelessly unless the Sino-Russian relationship takes a turn for the better.

Now, her relations with America and the West in general: As we saw in the Poplar Tree Incident in Panmunjom last year and in the recent shooting down of an American helicopter, tension still exists along the 38th Parallel between America and North Korea. North Korea is also deeply in debt to European countries. Her diplomats were involved in scandals and have been disgraced. North Korea's foreign relations are virtually stalemated.

This stalemate inevitably affects her internal politics, and she has been forced to backpedal from the radical strategy spearheaded by the "Three Great Revolutions Committee." I think the north won't be able to overcome her economic crises until she retraces her steps to the days before the time of the Three Great Revolutions Committee.

Kase: I should mention her policy for achieving an economic independence. Kim Il Sung gives the following explanation for North Korea's inability to redeem her foreign debts: Because of the recession in Japan, West Europe and America, North Korea has been unable to export what she had expected to. At the same time, charterage went up. This is why she has been unable to clear up these debts.

But charterage goes down when business becomes dull, and what Kim said is in error. More importantly, I question the soundness of a socialist economy that goes broke when the free world suffers a business setback.

Yajima: The North Korean economy has reached the stage where it cannot depend totally upon China and the Soviet Union. These two Communist countries themselves are in need of foreign loans. They promise, but are unable to honor the promises and offers of aid to North Korea. Therefore, North Korea must open relations firstly with Japan, West Germany and Belgium, and then with the Scandinavian and other free world countries.

Even now North Korea finds herself involved in the world economic mechanism and her ideology of *juche* is shown to be an ill-fitting one. The major commodities that North Korea can export are iron ores, cement, non-ferrous metals and various minerals.

Kase: Mostly raw materials.

Yajima: The prices of these export items, which are subject to the fluctuations of the world commodity market, plunged because of the widespread recession.

North Korea was over enthusiastic about catching up with the South Korean economy and impulsively imported machine plants and others in huge quantities. The amount of her imports soared while the prices of her export items declined sharply. There developed an ever widening gap between the two. This drove North Korea to the wall and she has had to default on the payment of her debts. Once in the mechanism of the world economy, her self-reliance-centered ideology of *juche* cannot hold water.

Tamaki: Some time ago, the editor of the *Yomiuri Shinbun* visited the north and the conversation he had with Kim Il Sung was reported in the paper. Their talk included considera-

144

tion of next Seven-Year Development Plan. The goals of the new plan were set far lower than the ten major goals of the preceding Six-Year Plan. Also the principle of self-reliance was stressed anew. In other words, there seems to be a tendency to withdraw into the shell of self. As Mr. Yajima noted, North Korea has experienced bitter setbacks in her initial encounter with the mechanism of the capitalist economy and so emphasizes developing a self-reliant economy. Possibly this will lead her to become totally isolated society. It's more dangerous.

Food shortage worsening

Kase: North Koreans have experienced trials and errors in their economic policy, but they cling to their national goals. They are hammering the so-called Kim Il Sung-ism into the people.

Ordinary life in the north is primarily characterized by "learning" or edification. Some Japanese intellectuals find this laudable, but Kim Il Sung's aim is to have all the children trained in state institutions under what he terms the "intellectualization of the whole people." Before a child reaches the age of 12 months, he is sent to a public nursery. He comes home in the evening. It is the same with kindergarten pupils and older children. The pattern of family life has been changed drastically.

Fukuda: That's the Spartan way.

Tamaki: At the Fifth Congress of the Korean Workers' Party, the theme of "Three Technical Revolutions"[8] was brought up. One of the three major efforts was to free women from as many household chores as possible. In order to achieve this, cooking, which takes up so much time and effort,

8. The Three Technical Revolutions are aimed at narrowing the gap 1) between heavy and light labor, 2) between industrial and agricultural work, and, 3) at freeing women from as many house chores as possible.

was to be communized. First came the joint preparation of side dishes. Later "rice factories" (communal food preparation centers) were established to cater for the entire community.

Kase: When North Koreans get up in the morning, they go to the "rice factory" for boiled rice and to the "side dish factory" for side dishes or secondary food. It's no longer necessary to do cooking at home.

Tamaki: It's said that all the cooking utensils have been taken away from the homes.

This story is seemingly about Pyongyang, and we don't know how they deal with this matter elsewhere. According to an official announcement, the average wage is 70 won per month. As the exchange rate is about 2 won for the dollar, the wage is equivalent to about 35 dollars, or 8,450 Japanese yen, the dollar being equivalent to 270 yen. Some say that the average wage has been raised to 90 won during the recent Six-Year Plan, but this is not confirmed. Seventy won is paid to the worker in Pyongyang, a model city where a preferential wage scale is in force. A short distance away from Pyongyang, however, a family barely scrapes together 40 won a month.

We say 70 won or 40 won, but there aren't any restaurants or eating houses. Nor are there coffee shops. Only some dining rooms or cookshops for high-ranking party cadres. There a bowl of vermicelli is served for 3 won and a bottle of liquor for 20 won. Such is the case.

The problem is that a rationing system is being applied to food and all other commodities. If a worker doesn't work at the factory every day, he cannot get ration coupons. Unless one has coupons one cannot eat or buy anything, no matter how much money one may have.

Rations are differentiated. An ordinary worker gets 600 grams a day; in Pyongyang the ration includes a half-and-half mixture of rice and other grains; in rural areas the ratio is 30 percent to 70 percent; high-level party cadre members receive the 100 percent rice ration.

As the food shortage has become acute since 1973 or 1974, each worker is asked when the monthly ration coupons are distributed, "How much food are you ready to donate to the state?" He is reminded that on the average 6-day rations are donated per month. He takes the cue and agrees to donate 6 days of rations. Then comes the question, "Where is your patriotism? Can't you raise the amount?" As the party cadres shout, the faint-hearted concede 10-day rations. So what such a worker actually receives is woefully inadequate.

To make up for rice shortage, an ersatz mixture of maize flour and other ingredients has been developed. This is called "okmi," and okmi factories have sprung up in every locality. Okmi resembles rice in shape but obviously is lacking in food value, for we often hear reports of the prevalence of pellagra due to malnutrition.

Kase: It's serious.

Tamaki: More serious is the fact that vivacity has disappeared from the daily lives of the ordinary citizens. They never engage in a lively conversation or make merry while eating and drinking in downtown places. Particularly in Pyongyang, people seem haunted by something and move around separately even on holidays. Families are seen walking around by themselves carrying no lunch baskets. People fish along the river, but never in groups.

If a man comes under the watchful eyes of the secret police, he may be in danger of being expelled from Pyongyang. To be sent out of Pyongyang means great trouble. One's living conditions become worse and one's record is indelibly stained. It's critical. Something is fundamentally wrong with this lifeless society.

Kase: North Korean news reels show that without exception Kim Il Sung and the party leaders are fat and healthy, but that the ordinary people are lean and skinny.

Tamaki: I met a man—a Korean—who had been to North Korea. As he insisted that he stop at Japan and say something about the north, I received him. He said there are two types of people in the north. One has a bright complexion, is well-built and wears stylish clothes. The other consists of the ordinary people whose complexions are pale, who wear tattered clothes and who walk with downcast eyes. These two types of people really live in quite different societies.

Fukuda: How about soldiers?

Tamaki: Maybe they can be divided into the two groups. Recently a young North Korean soldier fled to the south because he couldn't stand the starvation in the north.

Yajima: At Panmunjom, you see that the South Korean soldiers have light complexions, but that the faces of the North Koreans are black as if they had been tanned for 10 or more days on the beach.

Tamaki: I heard that one of the symptoms of pellagra is a sickly and dark complexion.

Yajima: The North Korean complexions reflect the food problem. They are not simply tanned during military exercises. South Koreans are busily engaged in maneuvers, too.

Kase: I read an AFP article in which it was stated that when a foreign ship arrived in a North Korean port, people came and begged for food.

Yajima: The drive to donate the staple food rations began when the oil crisis hit. Had the North Koreans been given sufficient food to be able to donate 10-day rations to the state prior to this crisis? Definitely not! This means the people are on the verge of starvation.

Old folk and children have organized a kind of a shock troop to pick wild ginseng and pokeweeds in the mountains for food. I think they are teetering on the brink of starvation.

148

People depend on blackmarketeering for a living

Tamaki: I also heard from a man who had been to North Korea that blackmarketeering is prevalent along the Eastern Coast, especially in such cities as Hungnam and Hamhung. They live by blackmarketeering. Otherwise, they can't live.

The man has a nephew in the north. The nephew wrote him: "Uncle, send me a car when you go back to Japan. Not an ordinary car but a coupe." "What for?" Then the answer came: "Sell it in the blackmarket." The man inquired where the blackmarket was and was told that it was in China beyond the Tumen River.

Fukuda: When did we Japanese experience that sort of living standard?

Tamaki: In 1945 or 1946 immediately after the war, so far as food is concerned.

Yajima: I think the situation in the north is worse than that. After the war, the Japanese said to themselves: "Hold on. Make one more effort, and we can get over this." They had a ray of hope? Do the North Koreans think in the way we did? No, they have no hope.

Fukuda: We did have the problem of undernourishment then, but the situation was not so serious as to make the complexions of half of the Japanese look as bad as those in North Korea today.

Kase: About 6,000 Japanese women went to the north with their Korean husbands. Our Ministry of Foreign Affairs officials say that many of them still have Japanese passports. But they aren't permitted to come to Japan for a visit. I read 50 to 60 letters that these women wrote to their families in Japan. Letter paper, particularly the latest ones, is of extremely poor quality. I was a primary school boy when World War II ended, and the writing paper resembles that in the notebooks I used at that time.

In the letters, the women asked for saccharine, medicines and such things. If the Japanese had written such letters just after the war, they might have asked for the same things.

Tamaki: There are three favorite articles among black-marketeers. They are watches, medicines and textile goods. All of them made in Japan. So the Japanese wives and their husbands write to their relatives asking for medicines when they are sick or for watches by the dozens to sell in the black-market.

Fukuda: Watches are a luxury. Is food adequate since it isn't included among the favorite items?

Tamaki: They smuggle in food from China and else-where.

Takase: But I don't think the food situation is good enough either in the Soviet Union or China.

Yajima: It's absolutely certain that food comes from China. The granary of China was once the area south of the Yangtze River, but now Manchuria produces the greatest amount of grain. Food blackmarketeering with Manchuria is a matter of common knowledge. Chinese living near the border, from Antung to Mukden or Shenyang, are able to trade their food for the goods they need.

Takase: The north is really in trouble.

Fukuda: If you were the Great Leader, what remedy would you offer?

Takase: Since Mr. Yajima is an economist, perhaps he has prescription. But I think that if the economy is in such an abyss, recovery won't be easy.

Kase: They may be tempted to start a war.

Tamaki: Or they could admit all the faults that exist in their economic planning and basically change their economic policy to adapt to the international community. Today, their products in every sector are poor. This is a decisive weakness. They should improve their industrial management and turn out products that are salable abroad. Also they should strive to improve seeds to increase food products. If they don't solve these basic problems one by one, they can't deliver themselves from this pitfall.

Fukuda: The easiest solution would be to cut the military budget.

Tamaki: That's right.

Fukuda: But they are afraid of doing that. They are out to liberate the south.

Takase: The central point is they are hard put financially. Even if they try to basically reform their industrial and agricultural policies, as Mr. Tamaki suggests, they will face many difficult problems in securing financial and other resources. From what we have discussed, I have come to understand the reasons why the north is unable to hammer out a long-range plan.

Yajima: The proportion of defense spending in the GNP is usually limited to 18 percent to 20 percent. North Korea's military budget is said to be about 15 percent, but, when the GNP falls, it easily jumps to 30 percent or so to maintain the present level of spending—crossing a crisis point. In that case the first thing to do is to curtail military spending. If they can't do that, the dinner plates of people are bound to be severely affected. But there are limits to that. What is the next option? They may start a war or accept whatever terms are offered by a foreign country. This is the ultimate choice left for the north.

In view of this, I am very embarrassed by the Japanese way of thinking. Pro-North Korean firms in Japan conduct their transactions only with the north. Mr. Utsunomia Toku ma, a member of the Diet who deserted from the Liberal Democratic Party, is advocating an equidistant diplomacy. He talks about equidistance, but the north and the south are not the same distance away.

Very recently, a certain firm in Japan and another in America simultaneously placed orders with sock manufacturers in South Korea for supply of socks for ten years. These Korean firms found it hard to meet these orders. South Korea's exports will probably amount to 10,000 million dollars this year—the amount that Japan attained ten years ago, in 1967.

Fukuda: Ten years ago, Japan enjoyed a high growth rate.

Yajima: Yes, she did. In Korea, the current balance of transactions including invisible exports, will go into the black either this year or next year at the latest. South Korea thinks it awkward to go into the black now, she is perhaps contemplating up-valuing the won before thie happens.

So it's hard to understand some Japanese politicians, scholars and intellectuals who are applying the same yardstick to the north and to the south and are trying the equidistance approach.

Fukuda: Newspapers, too, fail to report the difference between the north and the south.

Indoctrination halts production

Yajima: About ten days ago, I heard that South Korea is exporting black and white TV sets. But, actually, she has sold 50,000 color TV sets to America. While Japan is pottering about, some people fear, South Korea's color TV sets will make their steady inroads into the American market.

Fukuda: One of my relatives bought a high-class suit in America and found it was made in South Korea. South Korea sends the cloth in quantities to America and has it made into clothes there—though the design is presumably made elsewhere. This is but one example. Very recently, *Newsweek* (June 6, 1976) carried a feature story under the heading, "The Koreans Are Coming!" The economic advancement of South Korea is becoming a world-wide topic.

Kase: Before we shift our subject to the south, I'd like to tell more story about the north. According to the account of Mr. Makieda Motofumi of *Sohyo* (The General Council of Trade Unions of Japan), life in North Korea breaks down into 8 hours for working, 8 hours for "learning" and another 8 hours for sleeping. Refugees from the north have also testified that they worked 8 hours, slept 8 hours and spent the remaining 8 hours learning at their places of employment. They come back home around 11 o'clock at night.

Tamaki: Maybe it's a little too much to say that 8 hours are for learning. But, basically, they are duty-bound to spend 2 hours for learning at the places of employment.

Takase: What do they learn?

Tamaki: Learning about the ideology of *juche*! They learn by heart what Kim Il Sung has said and strive to cite his words fluently.

Takase: Japan did the same thing during the war.

Kase: The papers in the north have no space for social news such as fires, burglaries or other events. And the space is devoted to learning. Even the radio doesn't broadcast any radio plays or music programs as is done in our society. All hours are devoted to learning. Therefore, the whole country has become a school.

Yajima: The armed forces are the same. They are the same throughout the country, be they schools or military units.

Kase: The average worker lives in an apartment the size of 2-DK (2 rooms with a dining room-kitchen) in Japan. Photos of Kim Il Sung and, recently, of his son, Kim Chong Il, hang in every home. Every morning children get up to face the pictures and say, "Father, I thank you today as I did yesterday." So they are living not in a home but in a church.

Tamaki: The north's privileged guests may not know what is really happening there, but the journalists, business representatives and engineers accompanying exported manufacturing plants who go there do know what is really happening. We hear interesting stories from them. When North Koreans were asked what bothered them most, some of them answered cooly: "The house rent is low and we can manage to eat. But we hate the learning most."

Takase: They do learning so much. But I heard from a person who had been to the north for settlement of accounts. He said the North Koreans are poor at accounting. As their knowledge of export trade is virtually zero, he had difficulty in settling the accounts. So learning is ideological indoctrination after all.

Tamaki: So foreigners become sick of them. I also heard this from an engineer. As he worked in a factory in which a plant from Japan had been installed, he had ample opportunity for observation. Party members attended meetings very often and sometimes had to leave the factory suddenly. Once the party members had left, all the workers ceased to work. Everybody took a rest. (*Laughter.*)

Kase: I think I can understand them.

Tamaki: They cannot but take a rest. And productivity doesn't improve.

Takase: Regarding their factory management system, I can say this. Collective leadership has become established in the party apparatus. As no individual guidance is offered, they have become completely accustomed to collective leadership. Over them is a Party Committee. I think this is the first characteristic.

The second characteristic is that every economic operation is based on a political operation. Politics precedes and dominates economic activities. From this derives the supremacy of ideology or thought.

Thirdly, North Korea takes the so-called "mass line." The minority rules the majority as a system—I think it's also true of China. The minority very tactfully controls the majority. The blinder the masses, the easier it becomes to manipulate them. The apparatus is so designed.

And a centralized command system emerges as economic management system. A command or order comes from the Central People's Committee that in turn looks to Kim Il Sung as its highest leader. As a result, Kim Il Sung-ism has been established as the one and only guiding ideology.

This is the cardinal principle. But it is doubtful whether this principle can hold if and when the situation worsens so as to raise real issues. Conversely, it can be said that the centralized system has an advantage in that it can force its way through the masses. What do you think, Mr. Tamaki?

Tamaki: That principle no longer holds. That it has become estranged from the masses characterizes the North Korean politics of the 1970's.

The "Three Great Revolutions Campaign," [9] which was initiated in 1973 and has since produced warlike tension throughout the country, is aimed at the masses and senior

9. The Three Great Revolutions comprise: 1) the ideological revolution to arm the people with the *juche* ideology, 2) the technical revolution to introduce mechanization and automation in all sectors of the economy, and, 3) the cultural revolution to equalize cultural and living conditions between urban and rural communities, to improve cultural and scientific research and to combat the corrosive influence of non-Communist ideologies.

party cadres who have sided with them. The campaign was meant to put a new life into them and to reform them spiritually. The "Three Great Revolutions Circles"[10] which spearhead the movement are led by Kim Chong Il, Kim's son. His emergence as the highest leader in this movement was very ill-timed and awkward.

Several years ago, Kim Il Sung addressed a conference of agricultural workers. I was very surprised when I read the text of the speech. He cautioned in part: "When the work is over, you should wash your farming appliances clean so that they can stand long use." This means that the machines, implements and tools had been handled carelessly not only on farms but in factories, and so much so that Kim Il Sung felt compelled to deal with the matter personally.

Also in the same speech, he observed: "In rural communities the custom still persists that on ceremonial occasions people gather together and feast. This isn't the right thing to do. Make your ceremonial occasions as simple and frugal as possible." In present-day North Korea, people have a unique opportunity of enjoying themselves openly only on these ceremonial occasions. But Kim is trying to put an end to that, too.

Anyway, it is an abnormal situation when the highest executive of a country butts into such minor facets of daily life. There must have developed among the masses a tendency not to be submissive and to go their own ways. So Kim Il Sung found it necessary to invoke the authority of the Chief of State to deal with this. Gradually, he has come to concern himself with the minor details of the routine life of the masses. This has recently become another characteristic of North Korean politics.

Kase: Is politics of terror necessary under the circum-

10. The circles comprise 30 to 50 party members each and are dispatched to each factory, collective farm and others to carry out the Three Great Revolutions. The circles total 30,000 in all and report directly to the party headquarters.

stances?

Yajima: Naturally so. No other alternative is left.

Fukuda: He could follow Stalin's footsteps.

Tamaki: But there aren't left any rivals to purge.

Takase: His population, being but 16,000,000, is easy to control.

Fukuda: Do you mean that the only rival remaining is President Park Chung Hee? (*Laughter*.)

Politics, the economy, and ordinary life in South Korea

The Park Chung Hee Government and prosperity in the 1970's

Tamaki: Let me briefly sketch the situation in South Korea. In April 1960, there occurred a student uprising and a year later a *coup d'état* was staged. Since then Korean society has been a vigorous one. But intellectuals of *Yangban* (noble) lineage felt antagonistic toward the military coup. Originally, the *Yangban* society was ruled by scholar-statesmen and civil service was superior to the military service. During the period of Japanese colonial rule, the *Yangban* became submerged but came to life again when Rhee Syngman showed up in the wake of Japan's defeat.

Yangban supremacy was destroyed by the military coup and the intellectuals of *Yangban* lineage were antagonized. The Park Government was originally a military regime that came to power after the student uprising in 1960, but it has since given top priority to economic policy, not to military policy.

President Park has recruited men of ability in large numbers, men of both *Yangban* and *Sangmin* (commoner) origin. He doesn't care about their social backgrounds. In the traditional Korean society of former times, the upward mobility of the *Sangmin* was exceptional. Park has succeeded in fundamentally transforming the 500-year-old social structure of the Yi dynasty (1392 –1910).

Since President Park received his education at the Japanese Military Academy, he switched from a policy of leaning one-sidedly toward the U.S. by normalizing the relationship with Japan. He looked to Japan and West Germany as models and began to import not only their advanced industrial technology but their latest techniques in other fields.

This has resulted in the miraculous economic development of the latter 1960's and the 1970's. South Korea's achievements—especially those of 1969 and 1970—are spectacular. I think she achieved complete take-off then. More recently, I see a most drastic transformation wrought by the *Saemaul* (New Community) Movement—a reform movement in the rural areas—and in the opening-up of stockownership to the public—a movement for the democratization of enterprises, which the government has vigorously pushed since the world-wide recession in 1974.

These two movements have drastically transformed the traditional, stagnant *Yangban* society into a dynamic one. The intellectuals of *Yangban* lineage sensed a crisis and placed themselves in the van of an anti-Park movement. This dissident force is represented by former President Yun Po Sun and by Kim Dae Jung.

Upon whom do the dissidents rely? They rely on the Democratic Party in the U.S. and the American CIA which is close to that party. They started their movement banking on the support of the Americans and have become more and more dependent on the foreign support ever since. It seems to me that recent public opinion in Japan, and especially in Japanese pressdom, regarding the Korean problem has been manipulated by the American Democratic Party and the CIA.

Yajima: During the administration of President Rhee Syngman—that is, up to 1960—troubles occurred in rapid succession. One of the root-causes of these troubles can be explained as the price paid for construction of a free democratic country. Through 1950, the average growth rate was but 5 percent and the pie to share was small. This led to the outbreak of the student uprising as a result of which Rhee Syngman stepped down. Then came the John M. Chang Government.

The new government was democratic and pursued moderate policies. But it failed to hold in check the dissatisfied students and the populace behind them. Its democratic policy had its limits. In other words, the John M. Chang Government provides the lesson that the price of establishing a free nation is a high one and that the process should be a slow and gradual one. Now Major Gen. Park Chung Hee enters the political scene through a military coup.

Here I want to stress the point that economic development cannot be achieved without political stability. The Park Government is said to be a military regime, but it became a civilian government as the result of the presidential election held in the autumn of 1963. It is a historical fact that a firm basis for political stability has been constructed by the Park Government. Also significant was the normalization of relationship with Japan despite the Korean people's deep-rooted anti-Japanese feelings. President Park's patient and painstaking efforts finally culminated in the exchange of the significant ratification instruments on December 18, 1965. I agree with what Mr. Tamaki said.

Kase: Today, South Korea is regarded as a newly rising industrial power. At the time of the *coup d'état*, however, her per capita national income stood at a scanty 80 dollars. For comparison, that of Japan was about 1,200 dollars. What was most needed for such a poor country was to provide adequately for her people, to improve the welfare of the nation. To achieve that anywhere social stability is a prerequisite, as Mr. Yajima pointed out. Only on the basis of social stability can economic operations be conducted smoothly. As is seen in most developing countries, the government finds it necessary to force a certain degree of discipline on the people.

So we shouldn't forget that South Korea started with the per capita income of 80 dollars—though the papers both in Japan and America criticize South Korea as an undemocratic country.

Yajima: In this connection, I think it strange that the American papers responsible for molding public opinion in the U.S. do not have resident correspondents in South Korea. Without resident correspondents they cannot obtain firsthand news. I think that perhaps because of this, the real situation in the south is not reported as it is. I suspect that the *Washington Post* and the likes are presenting to America the image of South Korea as it is distorted in the Japanese papers.

Tamaki: They don't have resident correspondents in the south, but they do have CIA agents there. There is information that smacks of an American CIA touch. The Iwanami Shinsho series includes a book entitled *Kankoku karano tsushin* (Correspondence from South Korea) by an anonymous writer called "Mr. K.I." I think the report comes from the American CIA.

This book is a collection of articles that have appeared in the monthly magazine *Sekai* (The World). I was asked to review the book and so read it with care. Something is strange about the book. The basic tone throughout the publication is "the people in the south are miserable." As for the political situation, information drawn directly from inside the Korean Government and its intelligence agencies runs parallel with that gleaned from anti-government students and intellectuals. The channels of obtaining information and the attitude toward the people in the south are quite singular.

I became so suspicious that I contacted people who have long resided in Seoul and returned to Japan comparatively recently. I asked them who could supply such inside information, and was given to understand that there is a network of American CIA agents in Seoul. Most of these agents are highly-educated Korean intellectuals leading high-class lives. They engage in considerably risky operations, but they do so with impunity because the Americans have an understanding with KCIA. It's quite improbable that the KCIA doesn't have knowledge about the channels through which the reports are smuggled out monthly to Tokyo for publication in a popular magazine there. Only those who are in secure positions and free from arrest can do these things.

I also heard recently that these manuscripts are carried to Japan in American diplomatic pouches. Although I am not in a position to ascertain whether this is true or not, I think it's quite probable. The perception that " the people in the south are miserable" is the one that comes from people of high social status who look down on the masses. And it's quite an unwholesome approach to solicit support from abroad to salvage these "miserable people." From this, I conclude the writer or writers of this "correspondence" are extremely privileged beings in the south.

Kase: I'm amazingly surprised to hear that.

Fukuda: We discussed the press in Part I, and I also think America, including her CIA, is responsible for what the Japanese papers are today.

Kase: About 90 percent of American correspondents in Japan read English language papers published here, summarize the articles and then pass them on to America.

Fukuda: English language papers published in Japan are not so critical of South Korea as other Japanese papers, I guess.

Kase: Yes, they are very critical.

Yajima: American reporters recognize the Japanese as a

nation that uses Chinese characters. In this sense, they think we have something which they don't in so far as the China and Korean questions are concerned. So they read only English language papers in Japan and transmit rewrites based on them. I've heard about this, too.

Fukuda: What angers me is their impudence in thinking they can be correspondents in Japan without a knowledge of the Japanese language. How can correspondents from Japan, South Korea, Taiwan, India or any other country carry out their mission in America, England or France if they cannot read the papers published there or speak the language spoken there?

Kim Dae Jung does not represent the masses

Fukuda: Mr. Tamaki, do you think the American CIA gets its information independently without help from the Japanese?

Tamaki: I really think so. The American CIA has the stronger network of agents and is manipulating information in Japan.

Fukuda: That's what I think, as we discussed in Part I. Mr. Tamaki said the "Declaration for Salvation of Democracy" by Kim Dae Jung and others isn't the voice of the public, but represents a movement related to the traditional *Yangban* class. I think this fact is not perceived correctly by the CIA or by the leftwing in the American Democratic Party.

In Japan, there is a feeling that President Park is dictatorial and despotic. Most Japanese think Mr. Kim Dae Jung who opposes him is a champion of democracy, a friend of the masses who is promoting the cause of democracy. But, according to Mr. Tamaki's account, it is really President Park who represents the grassroots.

Tamaki: That's right. President Park does have closer

relations with the ordinary people. As viewed by the masses in Korea, the pro-American intellectuals are the privileged people high "above the clouds." They are genteel people whose hands are unsoiled by manual labor. President Park comes from poor peasantry and is congenial to the masses. He easily mingles with people in factories and on farms.

Fukuda: I went to Korea in 1975 and intuitively felt that. But most Japanese think the other way. It's a great problem.

Tamaki: The New Democratic Party is a group of intellectual elites of *Yangban* origin and is typically pro-American. The Korean mass media have changed to a great degree, but they—including the *Dong-A Ilbo*—represent these elites.

Yajima: So they are leaning to the opposition.

Tamaki: The Korean people are aware of that. They are highly politically conscious and often contending voices are heard even in rural homes during electioneering.

A husband, his wife and son often engage in a heated argument and thus decide for whom to vote. There's a tendency for the husband to support Kim Dae Jung while his wife and son support Park Chung Hee. It's a general drift. The aged husband is of an elite with Confucian tradition ingrained in him, and prefers Kim. This is a general trend in the rural community.

Yajima: Since the days of Japanese colonial rule, the south has been an agricultural region. What we called "the Korean rice" came from the south. The north is an industrial area.

So President Park decided to modernize and industrialize South Korea in the shortest possible time and has stressed an industrialization policy. As a result, the rural community fell behind and the erstwhile granary was forced to import about one million tons of grain annually. As a countermeasure, the *Saemaul* Movement was conceived to pave the way for a self-reliant rural economy.

Theoretically, an economic policy should be geared to the development of agriculture first and then to accelerating the growth in other sectors. But South Korea applied the theory in reverse: She has concentrated on industrialization first, making up for the food shortage with grain imported from America. As industrialization acquired a firm footing, Korea began to tackle the problem of modernizing agriculture and set in motion a drive for a self-reliant rural community.

Now, the country is entering a new era of heavy and petrochemical industrial development. This entails many problems. For example, the Dae Woo Machinery Industrial Company in Inchon has gone into the red, and the government provides funds to keep it afloat. In this way, the number of the enterprices under semi-government management has been increasing.

In principle, an enterprise is to be run initially under public management and then be transferred to civilian management when its footing has become secure. But South Korea does it in the reverse order. Because of the heavy and petrochemical industrialization policy, civilian enterprices ran into the red, and then the government intervened to provide funds. Thus orthodox economic theory has been bent a little. I think this characterizes the development process of the Korean economy.

Fukuda: It differs from the policy Japan pursued in the Meiji era (1868–1920).

Yajima: Yes. In the case of Japan, generally basic industries were placed under public management first and were transferred to civilian management when they had gotten into smooth running order. It was the reverse of the Korean policy.

Kase: In a sense, the Korean economic policy is in some respects socialistic.

Tamaki: Yes, it is. South Korea has had to proceed on the authority of the state to some extent. For example, consider the road construction that has provided the driving force for the economic development in recent years. South Korea has built extensive expressways and driveways. It has had to expand considerably the public sector in order to do so.

Fukuda: The construction of roads is intended, among other things, for military purposes.

Tamaki: That's right. But currently they serve as an expressway network for industrial and civilian transit, complementing the railroads. The role that the roads play in Korean economic development is great indeed.

Kase: Former Premier Tanaka Kakuei's *Thesis on the Remodeling of the Japanese Archipelago* wasn't popular, but it resembles the remodeling of the Korean Peninsula in that it proposes a systematic allocation of industrial estates throughout the country, estates which will be linked by roads.

Democratic "Saemaul" (New Community) Movement

Fukuda: Won't you tell us about the *Saemaul* Movement?

Tamaki: The movement began in full force in 1970. According to the Korean Government's official announcement, three honorably discharged veterans of the Vietnam war came back to a farm village in Kangwon Province and set about rebuilding their dilapidated community into a self-reliant one.

President Park took notice of this and at a gubernatorial conference gave instructions that this example be not only followed but expanded into a national movement. Thus was the *Saemaul* movement set into motion. To build new villages, they started off with comparatively simple projects: replacing straw-thatched roofs with neat **red- and blue-colored** tiled ones, or building community roads and bridges. In this way, people were motivated to join in the movement. Then they moved toward the goal of improving productivity by constructing community workshops and communal cooking centers. Villagers began to join hands in group work. To build roads and bridges requires funds. Here the government lends a helping hand, and provides such funds, not in full amount, but the amount of money which villagers are unable to raise by themselves.

Kase: Villagers raise a certain amount of money and the government provides a commensurate sum.

Fukuda: So the government is not forcing the movement.

Tamaki: No, it's not compulsory. The common benefits to be realized and the matter of spiritual reform are emphasized, however.

Kase: It is not coercive. On the contrary, villagers are encouraged to lift themselves up by their own bootstraps, and to heighten their consciousness of self-help.

Yajima: Behind the movement, there may be the motives of reconstructing the rural communities which were neglected during the 1960's when the emphasis was on industrialization, and of bracing up the dispirited farmers.

Takase: The north launched a similar movement called the *Chongsanni* work method[11] in February, 1960. It was a movement for the construction of new villages. It emphasized the "guidance on the spot."

It has something to do with the Seven-Year Plan. So I can say that movement and the *Saemaul* Movement came into being about the same time. The north professes to be working

11. A personalized, "on-the-spot-guidance" method or spirit allegedly developed by Kim Il Sung in 1960 during his visit to the Chongsanni Cooperative Farm in the north. It exhorts party and government functionaries to mingle personally with the farmers, help them find and solve their problems through comradely guidance. Also stressed is the provision of constant ideological guidance to the farmers to encourage them to make greater achievement.

from the grassroots, but orders do come from above. The *Saemaul* Movement in the south, however, sprang up from below. The two differ on that point, but were created around the same time. They must have been conscious of each other.

Tamaki: In terms of time lag, the south started ten years later. As I have said, the first motive of the south was to help the farmers make up for their communities which had seen left to lag so far behind during the period of successful industrial developoment. Another motive was the south's determination not to give in to the north whose collectivisation of farms was recording some initial successes. But the *Chongsanni* work method went overboard and failed.

Takase: Yes, the result shows that.

Tamaki: In the north, everything is under the absolute control of the party, from factories to cooperative farms. It's a completely artificial structure.

But, in the south, the Democratic Republican Party doesn't wield any power comparable to that of the Korean Workers' Party in the north. So, in the implementation of the *Saemaul* Movement—though I don't know what will happen in the distant future—they should depend on individual leadership to the fullest degree. It is still not clear to me what kind of people or what social strata are seizing the leadership in the movement. It will be necessary for Japan to send a study mission to find out about this.

Fukuda: Don't we know much about that?

Tamaki: No, we don't. We know only about the general results—that the South Koreans have attained self-sufficiency in food production and that the incomes of farming households have surpassed those of urban ones.

Kase: Our government source says that village chiefs may be standing in the van of the movement as it is said that the *Saemaul* leaders are public-minded villagers. But I think,

168

in many cases, that able leaders are chosen.

Yajima: Granted it sprang up from below, I think the movement initially resembled at some points the north's Flying Horse Movement[12] and the *Chongsanni* work method.

But, in terms of the process of organization, the *Chongsanni* work method is similar to the communes in China. As Mr. Tamaki has said, the Party controls every organization, allocates "work norms" and sees to it that they are fulfilled. When the "Three Red Banners" campaign,[13] started on the orders of Mao Tse-tung, failed in 1958, it was largely due to human factors—though the communes had suffered natural disasters as well. On this point the *Chongsanni* work method and the communes of China are very much alike.

Unlike them, the *Saemaul* Movement is more multi-purposed. Maybe they have come to think of multi-purposes—purposes other than those they first conceived of as the movement has progressed. For example, the levees of the Han River are being revamped as part of the *Saemaul* Movement to create jobs for farmers during the idle season. Another example is a job-creating public works program to absorb unemployed urban dwellers. Therefore, the movement has come to embrace many purposes: to motivate and rally the farmers as I have already noted, to increase their incomes and to create jobs for the unemployed.

Kase: The movement is under way not only in rural areas but also in the cities.

12. Named after the legendary Chinese flying horse, it is an intensive mass production drive began in 1959.

13. Proclaimed in 1958 in China as the guideline for China's future development, the policy included: 1) the General Line of Socialist Construction, emphasizing equally the development of heavy industry and agriculture and use of modern and conventional methods of production, 2) the Great Leap Forward to overtake England within 15 years, and, 3) the campaign to establish people's communes throughout China. Frank N. Trager & William Henderson, ed., *Communist China, 1949-1969: A Twenty-Year Appraisal* (New York: New York University Press, 1970), p.69.

Yajima: Yes, it is.

Fukuda: The *Saemaul* Movement has a broad spectrum of purposes. Even if leaders come from above in some cases, it differs from the *Chongsanni* work method and isn't coercive. People who aren't willing to join the movement cannot be thrown into jail.

Yajima: I've never heard of a man imprisoned because he wasn't willing to take his part in the *Saemaul* Movement.

Fukuda: Good-for-nothing fellows may be thrown out. That may happen, I suppose.

Tamaki: Rather, one who has failed to win the confidence of the people is alienated. In the case of the south, I mean.

Kase: It's a campaign for improvement of productivity, and for spiritual reform as well.

Takase: Wasn't this also so with the *Chongsanni* work method? According to official North Korean sources, the socialist reform was to have been concluded by 1958. The amalgamation of the cooperatives began in 1960. The *Chongsanni* work method emerged from that process. So the method had not only economic and agricultural aims, but other purposes as well.

Kase: You mean " learning " in short.

South Korea is not a dictatorship

Takase: It did include that—so that production could be linked with administration. As Mr. Yajima observed, it bears some similarity to the communes of China. Here North Korea's economic framework begins to reveal a shade of difference from that of the Soviet Union.

That similar movements turned up around the same time in the north and the south—be they from above or from below—is evidence that the rural areas provide the basis for nation-building. It also indicates that these two countries turned inward as the international situation deteriorated.

Fukuda: Mr. Takase, you seem to be taking lightly the matter of whether a movement is initiated from above or from below. It's the most important question.

Takase: We say it is started from below in the rural areas, but actually it's difficult for a movement to come from below. Even in the case of rural reform in Japan, they could do nothing without leaders.

Fukuda: It's not the question of leaders, but of whether the effort is instituted voluntarily or forcibly, of whether the government exercises its powers or not. This is the crucial point.

Today, Japanese newspapers and the Diet debate the fundamental question: Is South Korea free or not? Is she democratic or not? Does her government have popular support or not? So we have been most concerned about and have striven so hard to answer the question: Does the movement start from above or from below?

Takase: After all, the question will be answered by seeing through the difference in the fundamental characteristics of the political systems of the nations. The characteristics of the south and the north are distinguishable.

Fukuda: We know there is a difference between the fundamental natures of the two countries. But that fact isn't considered by most Japanese. They just say South Korea is dictatorial, is not a democracy and not to be counted among the free nations. That is also heard in America.

Takase: I think Mr. Fukuda thinks South Korea is democratic.

Fukuda: What I think is not important. What's important is whether South Korea really is dictatorial as is so often asserted in Japan and America. I think we should convey to our readers an accurate real picture of the south.

We have observed the difference between the *Chongsanni* work method and the *Saemaul* Movement. *Saemaul* better suits our taste. The *Chongsanni* work method goes against the principles of democracy. So the question of whether it started from above or from below can never be brushed aside as a trivial one. The difference does matter.

Yajima: During the war, Japan initiated a campaign for rural self-reliance and tried many things. But the campaign ended in disaster. It failed because it came from above.

But after the war, many popular demands, including those related to rural problems—such as the rice prices under the food control system—that came from below have transfused fresh and different political blood into government policies, setting aside the question of whether they are right or wrong.

Tamaki: A case of postwar success is the Federation of Agricultural Cooperative Associations. It wasn't imposed by the government though it reactivated the organization by enacting a law.

Fukuda: If the end justifies all, the ultranationalist Japanese army officers involved in the abortive military *coup d'état*, popularly known as the February 26 Incident,[14] can be exonerated.

Takase: I didn't mean that. I think the South Korean workers are very excellent. They are highly motivated and their strong will to work is a very important factor in the achievement of Korea's high economic growth rate. Compared with the workers of other Third World nations, their willingness to work is far stronger. I think this is the south's

14. An unsuccessful *coup d'état* staged by about 1,400 Japanese troops led by some young extremist officers on Feb. 26, 1936. The incident that killed or wounded some important government leaders resulted in placing the army in undisputed control of the affairs of state.

172

greatest merit.

But, seen from abroad, the Park Government has established an economic structure dependent upon export. It follows the so-called foreign capital inducing pattern. The Korean economy is linked to the external circulation structure—the so-called international equilibrium—rather than to the internal circulation mechanism. Its dependency on foreign countries is great.

This worked in the 1960's, but in the 1970's ever since the oil shock, the international environment has deteriorated. To take the example of food, South Korea has found it hard to rely totally on foreign countries. Her agriculture has been forced to turn gradually inward. The reconstruction of dilapidated rural areas is part of this. It was at this point in 1970 that President Park came to notice the *Saemaul Movement*. I think it has been promoted not only by the farmers, but actively by the government.

Yajima: That's natural. We have already talked about this. But the *Saemaul* Movement did come from below.

I have watched the recent development of the *Saemaul* Movement. Farmers' incomes are curving steadily upward. Although I don't have accurate figures, the population that concentrated in cities as the result of the industrialization policy, now shows a tendency to move back to the rural areas.

Tamaki: The trend has begun indeed. At least, the extreme concentration of people in urban areas is now being checked.

Yajima: That is one of the aims of the *Saemaul* Movement, and I think conditions are maturing, as Mr. Takase has pointed out, for the movement to play a role in inducing a domestic demand-oriented pattern of economy. This is an interesting point.

Tamaki: As you said, it's interesting that Korea has taken a course which is the reverse of Japan's. The south is creating a peculiar pattern of modernization that is different from the conventional one in many respects. If it succeeds, therefore, it will certainly have a great impact on other developing countries.

Yajima: Can I put it this way? The government routes a waterway and then lets the people flow the water for themselves. If water is in short supply, the government makes up the shortage. Isn't it designed roughly this way?

So South Korea is different from a country which instructs the people to route the waterway, to flow the water down and then cracks down on those who complain about a shortage of water.

Fukuda: The question is whether the people who don't strive are purged or not. This is what I am most anxious to learn.

Yajima: No purge at all in the south.

Fukuda: In the north, it is possible to crack down on or purge those who complain. I would say the northern regime is doing that now already. If we participants do not make this difference quite clear to our readers, this book won't be worth publishing. Newspapers are full of reports that South Korea is dictatorial, and their readers are half in doubt.

Takase: I agree with you on that point, but I am doubtful if it comes to the question of whether the south is completely free. I am also doubtful that things really come from below as you all have argued.

Fukuda: The same thing can be said about Japan. Is our economy operated through completely free competition? It's a government-managed one.

Takase: I know what you mean.

Fukuda: America is the same. An anarchist could claim that all the countries in the world are dropouts.

Yajima: As Mr. Takase said, history has its stages of

174

development. As the stages of development differ, so does the latitude of freedom. If we take the historical approach as Mr. Takase always argues we should, the latitude of freedom always presents a problem.

Takase: I understand.

Tamaki: When I think about the question of "freedom," we should first develop a basic yardstick for measuring it. Recently I have come to think that we should consider the basic question of how independently the working masses are able to design their own lives, manage them, preserve and fulfill them. We will be mistaken if we do not first ask ourselves this question.

Viewed from this angle, we can say that the latitude of freedom has since ancient times been considerably high among the masses in China, Korea and Japan, high enough to be a fair match for that in Europe. In the process of modernization, however, freedom has been eroded, limited and repressed in many ways. The latitude of freedom of a nation is determined by the ability of the people to resist and cope with this situation.

In this sense, the South Korean people are valiant indeed. While holding high their life principles, they ride the stream of modernization. Compared to this, the North Korean Government interferes with and controls every aspect of its people's lives. This has resulted in the loss of vitality as a viable society.

People are watching closely

Tamaki: I've encouraged young people who seem to have been baptized by Japan's new left to visit South Korea as soon as possible. Many who do say that South Korea is a far better country.

By that they mean the quality of public life is richer than

it is in Japan. The life in Japan has become urbanized, exigent, uniform and sleazy. In terms of food and living conditions, South Korea is more in harmony with nature and is a fine country with marked characteristics. Some Japanese are even willing to settle down there if that became possible.

Fukuda: Since I have visited the country myself, I understand that sort of feeling. Then why is it that South Korea is considered not free? Let's compare her with Japan and find out in what respects she isn't free. Mr. Takase said he entertains a doubt about the south. Won't you elaborate on this point?

Takase: There are many syndromes.

Fukuda: To be concrete?

Takase: It concerns the freedom of the press after all.

Tamaki: They have no freedom to stage demonstrations and carry on anti-government publicity.

Yajima: There are trade unions of various sorts, but a union movement is not permitted.

Tamaki: If we examine how the press and politicians are repressed, we find it is done fairly selectively.

It has become markedly clear during the past two or three years that the government cracks down on the dissidents who rely on what they term the "outside force," or influence of foreign countries. It represses Kim Dae Jung, Yun Po Sun, Catholics or others who try to overthrow the government on the strength of American or other international forces. Although many Protestant clergymen and laymen have engaged in anti-government activities, they are not cracked down as long as they don't capitalize on foreign connections. They are put in jail and then released. This is done very cleverly.

Fukuda: Ham Sok Hon, a leading dissident, was a

disciple of Uchimura Kanzo[15] and is a Protestant of the non-church movement.

Tamaki: Yes, he is. There is a slum area along the Chonggye-chon in Seoul; a Protestant pastor there is carrying on a movement for relief of the poor and against the government. The police arrested him but then set him free in less than a year. Once out of jail, he continues his activities. The pastor by the name of Kim Kam Hong has written a book. *Akatsukio yobisamasu kane* (A Bell Awakens the Dawn) which gives an account of this matter. We easily use the word "repression," but the South Korean Government applied it very selectively. The people are watching this closely.

Fukuda: I once met Mr. Kim Dae Jung and Mr. Kim Yong Sam, former President of the New Democratic Party. Referring to the matter of difference between them and President Park should one of them be elected to the presidency, I put a specific question: "Will you grant freedom of the press to Communists?" Both of them replied, "No."

Yajima: Be they Kim Dae Jung or Yun Bo Sun, they are thoroughgoing anti-Communists.

Fukuda: What do you think, Mr. Takase? Should Kim Dae Jung allow freedom of the press to Communists if he is elected President?

Takase: I am not in a position to answer the question as I haven't followed the case of Kim Dae Jung. But, speaking about President Park, I think he should be more responsive to international reaction.

Fukuda: In other words, he should be more attentive to the opinion of those around him and take it a little easy.

Takase: He can't do that because of the 38th Parallel. As long as the 38th Parallel remains, Western style liberalism

15. A religionist, critic and promoter of the non-church movement (1861–1930).

won't be realized. The same thing can be said about the north. As long as the national division continues, the south and the north will find themselves acting in ways that are inevitable—though the north is far more dictatorial.

Fukuda: To what readers in Japan are you saying that? Few Japanese intellectuals speak ill of the north.

Takase: I can't understand their position. Shouldn't they be more fair? Toward the north as well as to the south?

Fukuda: It poses a problem because they aren't fair.

Takase: That's right. They aren't. I feel that way.

Fukuda: Yes, certainly. Let's take the case of the three largest papers in Japan. They are simply not fair. Which do you think the Japanese press favors, the north or the south?

Takase: I think they probably favor the north.

Fukuda: Yes, they do. Because the Japanese newspapers don't perceive things fairly and the intellectuals lean toward the north, we have developed this program to correct their mistaken notions. So there isn't any need to justify the north.

Takase: That's why I am present at this meeting. I have many things to learn from this discussion.

Tamaki: You said President Park could modify his policies, and I think he must be inclined to do so. But he should not make himself appear to be yielding to the intervention of America and Japan in Korea's internal affairs. In view of the national sentiment prevailing in Korea, he cannot give the appearance of succumbing to external pressures. South Korea has progressed to that extent. I think President Park will gradually moderate his policies of his own accord and according to his own judgment.

Takase: I see.

Yajima: Another point is that the south has progressed into being a society with a high literacy rate, and an increasing number of intellectuals. Generally, the intellectuals tend to take an anti-establishment and pro-opposition position. Conditions are now ripe in the present-day Korea for the emergence of a vigorous dissident movement, for good or bad. This places President Park in a difficult position.

A Saudi Arabian King has much money in his coffers. But he isn't very enthusiastic about popular education, perhaps out of fear that such education will presage overthrow of his dynasty. But President Park's case is the reverse of this. And Park isn't clinging to power as is widely thought in Japan. More importantly, he is most concerned about the possible development of a situation, which could be worse than the current confrontation with the north.

Tamaki: The south has built a strong basis for national unification, far stronger than has the north.

Yajima: Yes, she has.

Tamaki: In a sense, I am sympathetic with the North Koreans. They have pushed too far the bad side of Marxism-Leninism, perhaps to the point of no return. I feel pity for them.

Fukuda: I understand how you feel.

"White Capitalism" belittles Asia

Yajima: It is a great tragedy for the people in the Korean Peninsula, both in the south and in the north, that the homogeneous nation was divided politically along the 38th Parallel.

Furthermore, the 38th Parallel is not a line to be brushed aside simply as "an illegitimate child" of the Second World

War. Looking back, we see Premier Yamagata Aritomo[16] proposing at the first Imperial Diet convened in Japan (November 29, 1890) that such a line be drawn in Korea as to separate areas to be controlled by Japan and by Korea—for protection of Japan's sovereignty and national interests. This line ran across present North Korea, from Pyongyang to Wonsan. It is along the 39th Parallel. And it's worth remembering that Korea was an independent country at that time. Historically, such has been the geopolitical location of Korea as to tempt Japan to seek a line for the protection of her national interest. We have to take this fact into consideration.

I should make one thing clear in this connection. In the past, Japan has often bullied both South and North Korea. Today an expiatory way of thinking probably underlies Japan's Korean policies. I am also inclined to think that this feeling is prevalent in the subconscious current of the ordinary Japanese people.

This is a grossly mistaken notion and nothing is more insulting to South and North Korea than this sort of thinking. Five or six years ago, we heard Koreans talking about such "villainous" figures or events of the past as Toyotomi Hideyoshi, Kato Kiyomasa[17] and the Japan's colonial rule of Korea (1910 – 1945). Rarely do educated Korean people mention the latter now. Their goal is to get on with Japanese as equals. To feel "compassion" or a need to "live down" will be making fools of the Koreans. We should not overlook this point.

Another thing. To a historian it is of course of primary importance to clarify the relationship between and among the

16. Yamagata (1861 - 1922), a general and statesman, when he signed a protocol with Russia (the Yamagata-Lobanov Protocol) in Moscow in the summer of 1896, was said to have proposed Russia to divide Korea into two parts along the 38th Parallel to be controlled by Japan and Russia. Loh Keie Hyun, "A Historical Study of Korean Division," *The Journal of International Law* (published by the Korean Association of International Law), Vol. 8, No. 1, March 1963, p.27.

17. Kato Kiyomasa was one of Toyotomi Hideyoshi's generals commanding the Japanese troops that invaded Korea in 1592 and 1597.

facts about each period of history. But the historian's task should not end there. He should then strive to see how the past is linked to the present, and what significance it has for our own time. This point is very important. I once read *The Historian's Craft* by Marc Bloch. He said that the basic task of the historian is how to link the past to the present.

You may wonder why I am talking about this. It is because it is imperative that we seek a "linkage" between the past and the present. To link them by expiation is unproductive. It certainly isn't salutary. Nations in conducting foreign affairs as equals should take a "forward look"—should try to link the present to the future. Relationships between equals aren't debtor-creditor relationships.

Tamaki: A Korean once told me to my face, "Japan is very cunning. Had she endured and chosen to fight on a little longer, a revolution would inevitably have taken place in Korea. (*Laughter*.) But she was cunning enough to give up fighting before this occurred. We were destined to suffer from this, for our country was then divided along the 38th Parallel." Now both of our two peoples should endeavor to create a climate which will enable us to engage in open-hearted, candid discussions.

Fukuda: It's indeed true.

Yajima: America miscalculated. She thought that the Japanese troops in Manchuria were invincible and that Japan would not surrender until 1946. As a result, the Americans worked to bring the Soviet Union into the war. But, by then Manchuria was empty, and the crack Japanese troops once stationed there had been sent elsewhere. On August 6, 1945, the Russians declared war on Japan and were already in Korea only three days later. This American miscalculation is attributable to the unhappy state of affairs in the Korean Peninsula.

Tamaki: Since the end of the Pacific War, America's

Asian policy has been full of bungles. Following the war, she ruled Japan indirectly through Japanese and tackled the problem of political reform. On the other hand, she established a military government in Korea, and didn't allow the Koreans to create their own reforms. American policy was mistaken from the start.

Yajima: So it was. The 38th Parallel became fixed by the Truman Doctrine. Then Secretary of State Dean Acheson announced that the American defense line in the Pacific ran through Guam, Japan, Okinawa and down to the Philippines. The Korean Peninsula lay outside that line. So Kim Il Sung visited Stalin twice and also met Mao Tse-tung. Mao, saying he would concede to Kim if America was to forsake Korea, authorized 25,000 Korean-Chinese troops under Lin Piao to cross into the north. These troops were followed by 50,000 volunteers, and Kim started the disastrous Korean War.

Now, President Carter is trying to draw the same defense line that Secretary Acheson did (thereby inviting the Korean War), and is also advocating the withdrawal of the American troops from Korea.

Fukuda: As was mentioned in Part I, President Carter gives as a reason for the proposed withdrawal that America defends Korea not for the sake of Korea, but for that of Japan. To say that is to slight the Asian people.

Tamaki: In a sense, yes. America is pulling out her troops from Korea to suit her convenience and is applying pressures upon Korea by raising the issue of human rights. This is quite hypocritical and self-serving. We would think it strange if Korean people did not become anti-American in the face of such an American attitude.

Fukuda: So it is a falsehood when she talks about morality or human rights. If America treated Asians as equals, she couldn't be saying such insulting things to the Korean people. But she can do that because America is prepared to say,

"Japan is necessary for defense of Europe. Japan is needed for checking the Soviet Union." In this respect, America is a wayward country.

Yajima: That's why I call the United States a white capitalist. Japan, South Korea and Taiwan enjoy her protection as long as they do not stand in her way. If they get in the way, they will be dumped. (*Laughter*.)

Kase: Wasn't it America that divided Korea at the 38th Parallel ?

Yajima: Yes, she did it.

Kase: The Soviet Union didn't do it. And the moral responsibility rests with America.

Fukuda: For all that, America is talking about moral diplomacy. I dare say she is a dissembler. But I should make it clear that, by America, I mean America in general, not individual American citizens. We have received research grants from many American foundations and have many friends and acquaintances in that country. (*Laughter*.)

Yajima: In ancient times, there once was a "preaching burglar" in Japan. America resembles him.

Fukuda: The withdrawal of the American troops from Korea is a sort of bluff.

Kase: I am on friendly terms with a high-ranking American Government official. He once said something to the following effect: Most of the people in the American Government believe America will have Japan at her beck and call as long as she depends on America for her national defense and security. America should be thankful that she has such a great power at her beck and call.

This official is an advocate of an alliance between Japan and America, but thinks that American Government leaders are only too willing to have Japan at their service.

Fukuda: Japan is a member State of the United States of America.

Yajima: Yes, she is.

Fukuda: So the Self-Defense Forces of Japan are like the American National Guardsmen.

Tamaki: But the National Guardmen are called out when a student riot erupts.

Fukuda: Oh, yes.

Tamaki: But Japanese Self-Defence Forces aren't. (*Laughter*.)

Kase: In that sense, South Korea is a far more independent country than Japan.

Fukuda: It's strange that Japan, nothing but a member State of the United States, should be saying this or that about South Korea, an independent country.

Tamaki: Koreans have a stronger sense of pride than the Japanese, and their hearts burn with a sense of mission. They receive aid from both America and Japan, but never allow themselves to become a dependency. They make the most of such economic aid and are determined to overtake and outrun their benefactors. If we take pity on Korea or treat her as a backward nation, we are bound to suffer repercussions.

Some Japanese intellectuals loudly criticize South Korea as though the country were still in the Tojo Hideki era. They are rubbing her the wrong way. How can they do that with *sang-froid*? I can hardly understand it. This may yet be another example of the tendency among the Americanized Japanese intellectuals to turn up their noses at the Koreans.

Yajima: South Korea finds herself in an ever deteriorating situation. A Carter-Mansfield line doesn't provide constructive plan for Asia.

Fukuda: I'll vouch for the soundness of your opinion with no reservation whatsoever.

Economic aid is one thing, "connection" another

Fukuda: As economic aid has come up in our conversation, I want to ask you about the matter of the "American-Korean *yuchaku* (connection or link)" and the "Japanese-Korean connection." This is someting people are making a great fuss about.

Kase: The terms "connection" or "link" sound strange. There are many Japanese business firms and Dietmen in the Liberal Democratic Party who are urging the promotion of friendship with socialist countries. In the cases of the firms clinging to China and the Dietmen friendly with the Chinese, the word "connection" is never used. Why is the term applied only to the relations with free countries?

Yajima: They talk about the Korean lobby or the Taiwan lobby, but never about the Pyongyang lobby or the Peking lobby.

Kase: Doesn't that reflect the basically prejudiced position that socialist countries are clean and that capitalist or liberal countries are dirty?

Yajima: I think so.

Tamaki: Recently a Korean visitor to Japan said that the term "connection" is fine. It means, literally, " healing " or " curing of a disease."

Fukuda: It's a medical term. Leucocytes are called out to fight and destroy the encroaching bacilli. In the process they dry up, adhere to the intestinal tract and remain in a secure, conglutinated state. In case the adhesion becomes excessive, it will have to be removed. But, generally, the "link" or "connection" has a good meaning.

So, in the *yuchaku*, leucocytes are called on to engage in

the good cause of saving a life. As there is no word *yu* (癒) in the government designated Chinese characters for daily use, it is spelled *yu*(ゆ) in *Kana* (the Japanese syllabaric alphabet), obscuring its original meaning.(*Laughter*.) In this sense, the American troops in Korea are to be strengthened and her economic aid to the south speeded up greatly. That's what the leucocytes are supposed to do in bringing about a state of *yuchaku*. In that process something undesirable may develop, but should be tolerated to some extent. In a severe case, there must be a second operation. But, originally, the expression had a good meaning as you said.

Kase: They make much ado about the Japanese-Korean "connection." But these two countries are neighbors and it's natural to help a neighbor. Of course, it's illegal and unjust for public servants to abuse their authority, and stuff their pockets, or to indulge in graft and corruption. But economic aid shouldn't be thought of as a "connection."

Yajima: Postwar Japan somewhat resembles the *Sung* dynasty(960–1279) in Chinese history. The dynasty totally ignored military preparations and devoted itself to economic construction. It used the expression "economic assistance," and gave money or silk cloth to many countries. Japan had no relations with the dynasty, but benefitted from its assistance.

Kase: Did they use the words "economic assistance" then?

Yajima: Yes, they did.

Kase: It's interesting.

Yajima: Japan's like the *Sung*. She does nothing but trade. So she should step up her economic aid. It's natural for her to provide economic aid to South Korea.

Fukuda: Few use the phrase Japanese-American "connection."

Takase: Reformists are using that.

Fukuda: That reminds me that the expression "sitting-on-the-fence-diplomacy" was once in vogue. But the anti-American sentiment has now become somewhat mitigated.

Kase: Ironically, where the anti-American lobby has its strongest foothold is America. (*Laughter*.) The lobby there seems to have been joined by anti-Americans in Japan.

Fukuda: Even the Japanese Communist Party has served their cause by demanding the scrapping of the Japanese-American Security Treaty. Being a slow learner, I have come to have an anti-American feeling only now. (*Laughter*.)

Tamaki: It's true of the South Koreans. They are anti-American. Young men who have received their higher education in America are returning home in large numbers. Some of them have been placed near President Park as his secretaries or special assistants.

Kase: You mean the graduates from colleges and universities in America?

Tamaki: They are watching the United States closely. They are doing so as if telling Americans, "I won't have you say so." They belong to the younger generation and so aren't in any way involved in the Japanese-Korean or the Taiwan lobbies of the past. President Park has replaced the members of his inner circles to a remarkable degree. So they are anti-American. They remain unruffled whatever stance the Japanese mass media or President Carter may take.

Fukuda: I wonder why the reformists in Japan join them and become anti-American when even such conservative reactionaries like me have become an anti-American. (*Laughter*.)

Tamaki: Basically, the reformist force in Japan has been fostered by the democracy that America sowed on Japan's soil after the war.

Fukuda: They were the trade unions who pulled in their horns when Gen. MacArthur made a dramatic appeal backed by his supreme authority to stop the February 1 (1947) strike—even though they had already declared a general strike against the government.

Tamaki: Because of the widespread existence of that sort of mentality, even the Japanese Communists acted foolhardily when the Lockheed scandal broke. They went to the United States to seek the benefit of being given some information about the case.

Yardstick for measuring freedom

Yajima: Now, let me take up a different topic. What always concerns me most is that there aren't any beggars in China or North Korea. But there are in South Korea. Some people in financial circles say that because there aren't any beggars in China or North Korea, these countries must be so much better off than South Korea.

Kase: In other words, full employment has been achieved there.

Yajima: But that's quite mistaken. A beggar resembles me in that he isn't engaged in any production. (*Laughter*.) Both of us are in the same trade. It's a tertiary industry. (*Laughter*.) The industry asks two things: Whether one is free to engage in that trade or is not free to do so. If you take up the beggar's trade in Tienanmen Square or in Pyongyang even for an hour, you will be taken somewhere and forced to work. Then the existence of beggars becomes a symbol of freedom.

Fukuda: Freedom to be a beggar is the highest freedom. It's greater than the freedom of the press.

Yajima: We should note another point. Beggars live off waste food, rummaging in garbage dumps or somehow picking it up elsewhere. Conversely, it means that people are so affluent as to be able to throw away leftover food. But they aren't that affluent—either in Pyongyang or Peking. The freedom to be a beggar and the freedom to throw out food—unless these two conditions exist, no beggars can exist. It's to be deplored that beggars don't exist in a country.

Fukuda: Therefore, whether or not a country enjoys freedom can be determined not simply by considering the freedom of the press, but by noting the existence or non-existence of the freedom to be a beggar, a loafer or a gambler. This is a far better yardstick for measuring freedom than is the existence or non-existence of the freedom of the press. But American puritanism doesn't recognize that.

Takase: As far as North Korea is concerned, the labor shortage is a great bottleneck in her economic effort. No man is allowed to be idle. And a socialist country forces labor upon its people.

Fukuda: In North Korea, the freedom to work or not to work doesn't exist. But it does in free countries.

Takase: The freedom of employment, you mean.

Kase: If an economy is open to the outside world and the people work hard, it is bound to grow. As we have noted, the north has a far smaller population than the south. Despite this, the north was originally an industrial region—while the south was agricultural—and so was in the better position to achieve take-off toward a mass consumption society. But she has failed to do so and now finds herself in an economic crisis because she has followed the line of a socialist command economy.

This is an important consideration when comparing the north and the south. Another consideration is the existence of freedom we've just discussed.

Tamaki: If the government tries to control every facet of the national life, the economy is bound to collapse.

Yajima: No socialist country is economically well off. To be specific, the Soviet Union and other members of COMECON (the Council for Mutual Economic Assistance) are suffering economically. They have borrowed about 43,000 million dollars from the West. This amount includes about 18,000 million dollars borrowed by the Soviet Union. Poland has also borrowed an amount equivalent to 20 percent of her GNP. Cuba's economic situation has recently worsened.

In Burma, the rice ration meets only one-third of the minimum requirement. The Burmese compensate by blackmarketeering. Teak, which was once a major export item, is unavailable now because it grows in the rebel-held area. Vietnam is in trouble. China is suffering. No socialist country including North Korea is economically prosperous.

Then what's important isn't making an academic comparison between Marxist economics and Malthusian or modern economics. I am not making a long-term projection, but currently the socialist economic system cannot but be judged one in which minimum living conditions cannot be achieved. Such achievement is possible only under a liberal economic system. I'm saying this on the basis of hard reality, not on any theoretical basis. Conditions prevailing in today's world must lead us to this conclusion.

Tamaki: I seriously question whether the nationalization *cum* monolithic planning *cum* collectivization that the Soviet Union has pursued ever since her creation is really a socialist policy. The Soviet policy may provide a temporarily effective technique when a developing country wishes to achieve rapid industrialization or militarization. But the technique's built-in faults will eventually surface. If a country continues to apply the method forcibly without thoroughly re-examining it and reforming fundamentally, she will eventually slide not only into economic stagnation, but into a reactionary political situation marked by purges, thought control and one-man dictatorship. I think that sort of mechanism is bound to move a country in that direction.

Koreans are not a whining people

Takase: I don't have any objection to that. But we should ask to ourselves whether the South Korean economic system is a perfect one. It's by no means perfect.

Tamaki: The south is also walking on a tight rope, and in the 1980's she will face another trial.

Kase: Do you mean that the South Korean economy will go broke because of the accumulated foreign debts?

Tamaki: Not that. The question is what will happen when her economic structure has reached a certain level and scope of development, and her social structure has been reorganized again.

New labor and social movements may develop. The *Saemaul* Movement may have to change its methodology. Whether the Park Government can effectively execute this task remains to be seen.

Yajima: In Korea, both prices and wages are soaring. A youth fresh from college is paid 140,000 to 150,000 won a month (80,000 to 90,000 yen). In this regard there is almost no difference between our two countries. So the south can no longer compete because of her low wages. She will also have to meet the problem of international payments.

Another weakness in the Korean economy is that its financial mechanism isn't sufficiently modernized—though this is a matter of degree. Interest rates were close to 30 percent in the 1960's and early 1970's, and there was a time when 27–28 percent was paid even on time deposits. This is very unusual. The fund shortage was given as the reason, but the financial mechanism will have to be modernized. Otherwise, an imbalance between the money and commodity flows will develop. We should pay careful attention to how the Park Government will meet this problem.

Tamaki: Another weakness is its technology. South Korea has continued to introduce advanced technology and seems to be moving very efficiently on the surface.

But she has the problem of unbalanced technology. At a certain stage, this will become a decisive weakness. In steel production, for example, slight changes in the hardening technique may result in a serious technological lag. This will weaken Korea's international competitiveness. So the technological gap in basic fields must be filled. In other words, South Korea faces a situation calling for a decisive raising of the general technological level. This, however, cannot be achieved in a day.

Takase: I should make some comments on what both of you have observed. As long as the world economy continues to expand greatly—as in the 1960's—the Korean economy will advance smoothly. But it will be difficult for the world economy to maintain high-growth rates in the future. Both North and South Korea have economies which are highly dependent on foreign countries. This will continue to pose a great problem—though I am not stressing only its adverse effects.

Kase: As some American experts have pointed out, the alleged weakness of the Korean economy is that the country has incurred one debt after another. Eventually, it will be impossible to repay the money and the country will simply become bankrupt.

But the same criticism was levelled at Japan when she was recording high economic growth rates. Today the GNP of the world is increasing each year and so is the pie to share.

Takase: No worry as long as the world economy continues to enjoy an expansionist trend. But a low-growth period may

192

lead into another period of government-managed trade.

Kase: I think the expansionist trend will continue.

Yajima: I think South Korea will be all right even in a low-growth age because she is physically strong. For instance, let's imagine a time has come when the Middle East has ceased to supply oil. Middle East countries are exporting oil for many purposes such as military preparations, industrialization and so forth. So their oil continues to flow into OPEC.

If the Middle East gives up and stops supplying oil—though this is most unlikely—all advanced countries will suffer severely. All will be forced to reduce their output, not merely slow down in the pace of growth. When governments are forced to appeal to their people to lower their living standard by 20 percent or 30 percent, the only nation that is ready to respond positively to such an appeal is South Korea. She isn't a whining and complaining nation.

Fukuda: That's what I have wanted to say.

Yajima: The Japanese will probably come up with a multitude of opinions and proposals and the result will be no action at all.

Fukuda: South Korea could successfully endure. Once the American troops are gone, President Park will find his job the easier. He can turn a misfortune into a blessing. Should I send him a cable of felicitation? (*Laughter*.)

Appendices

1. Chart of government structure of the south
   —Executive branch—

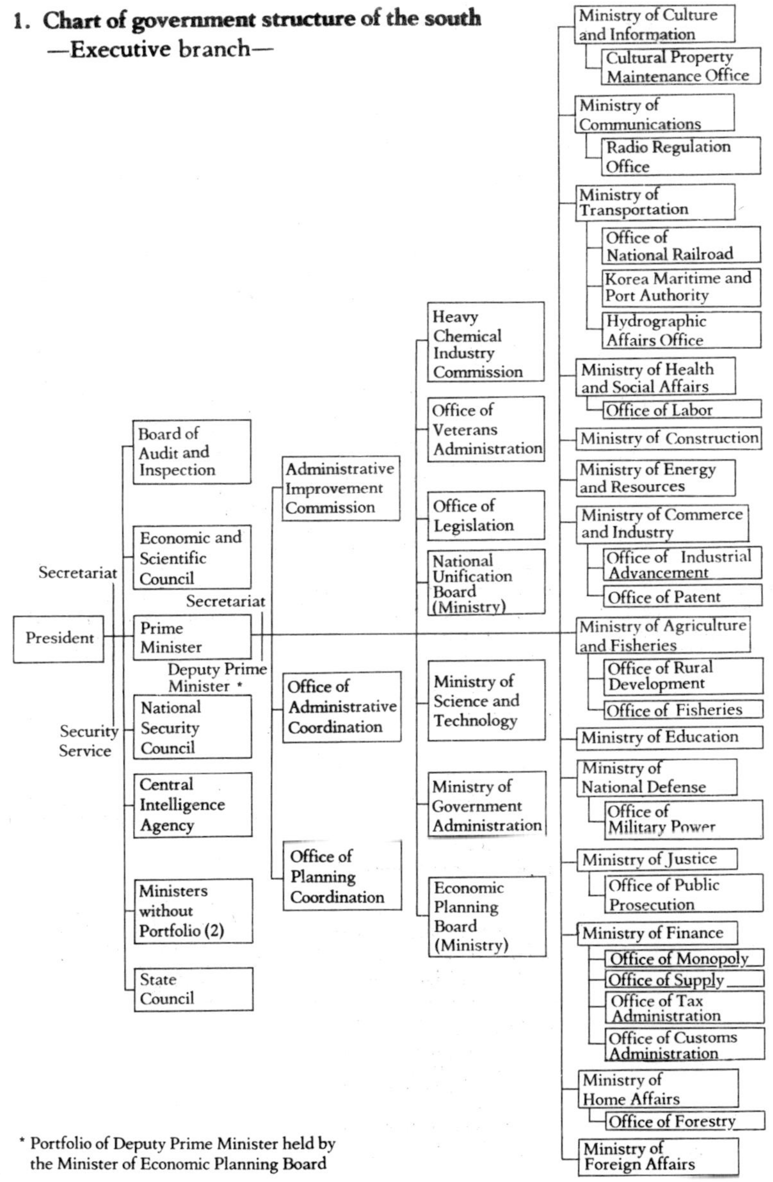

* Portfolio of Deputy Prime Minister held by
the Minister of Economic Planning Board

2. Chart of government structure of the north

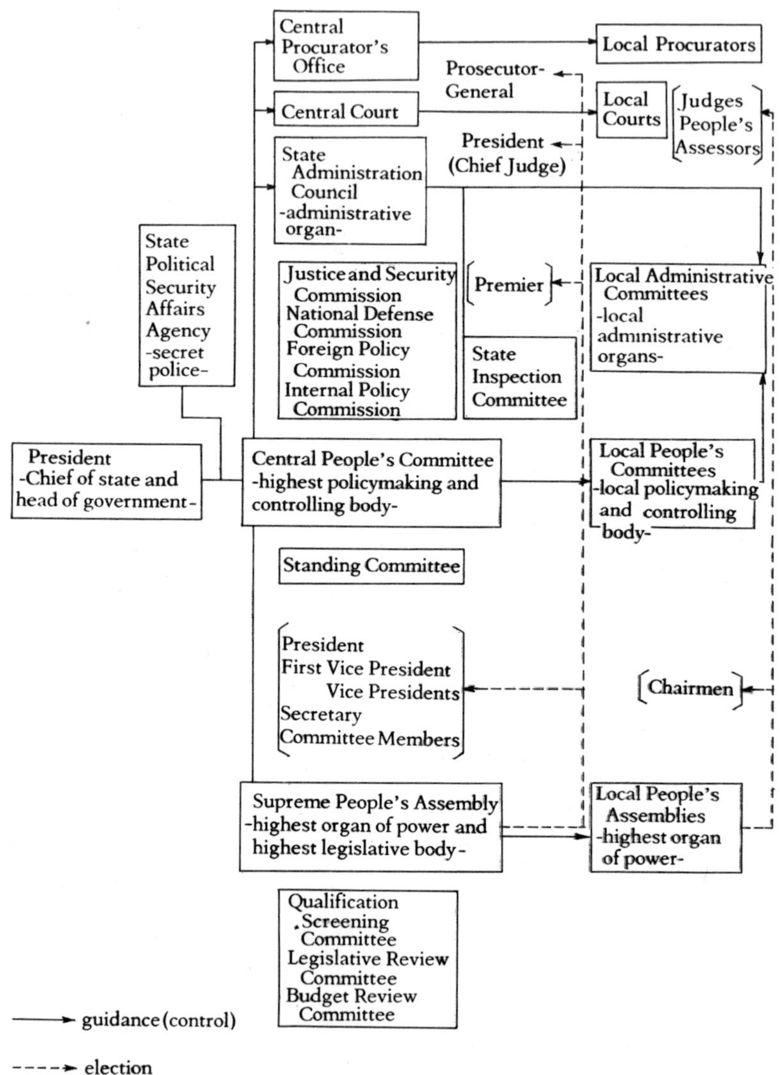

3. Defense and military organizational chart of the north

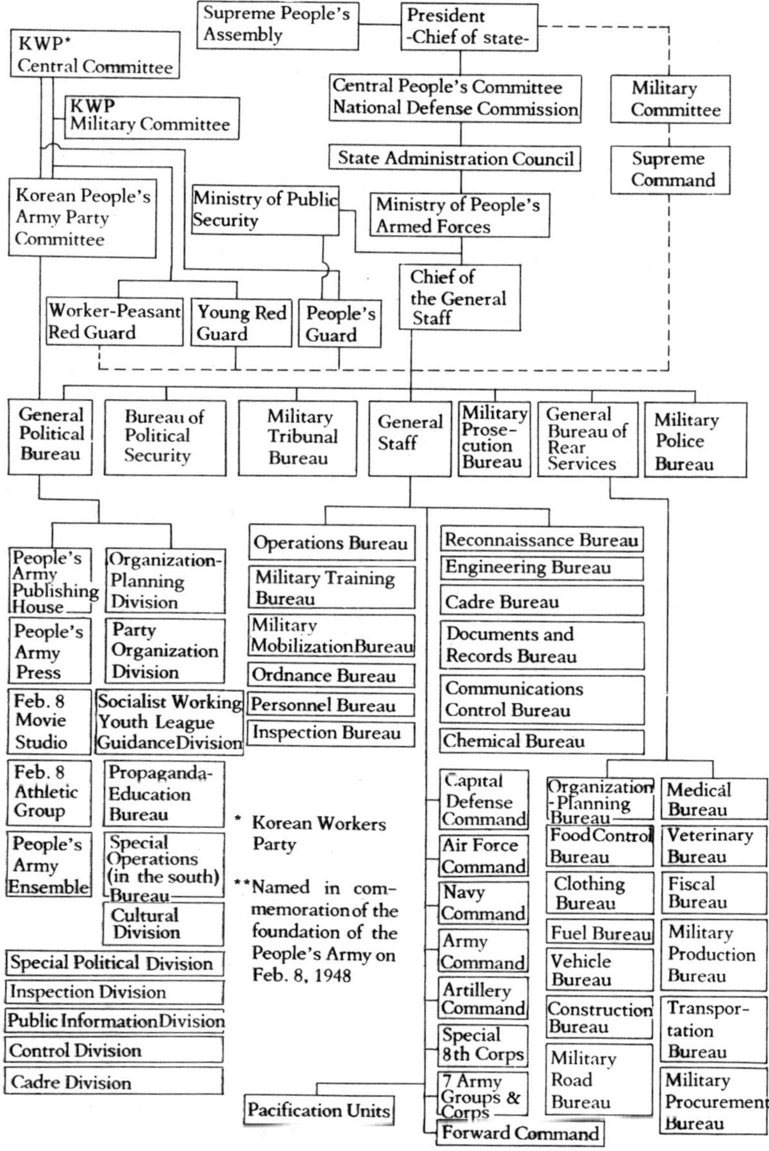

4. Genealogy of Kim Il Sung

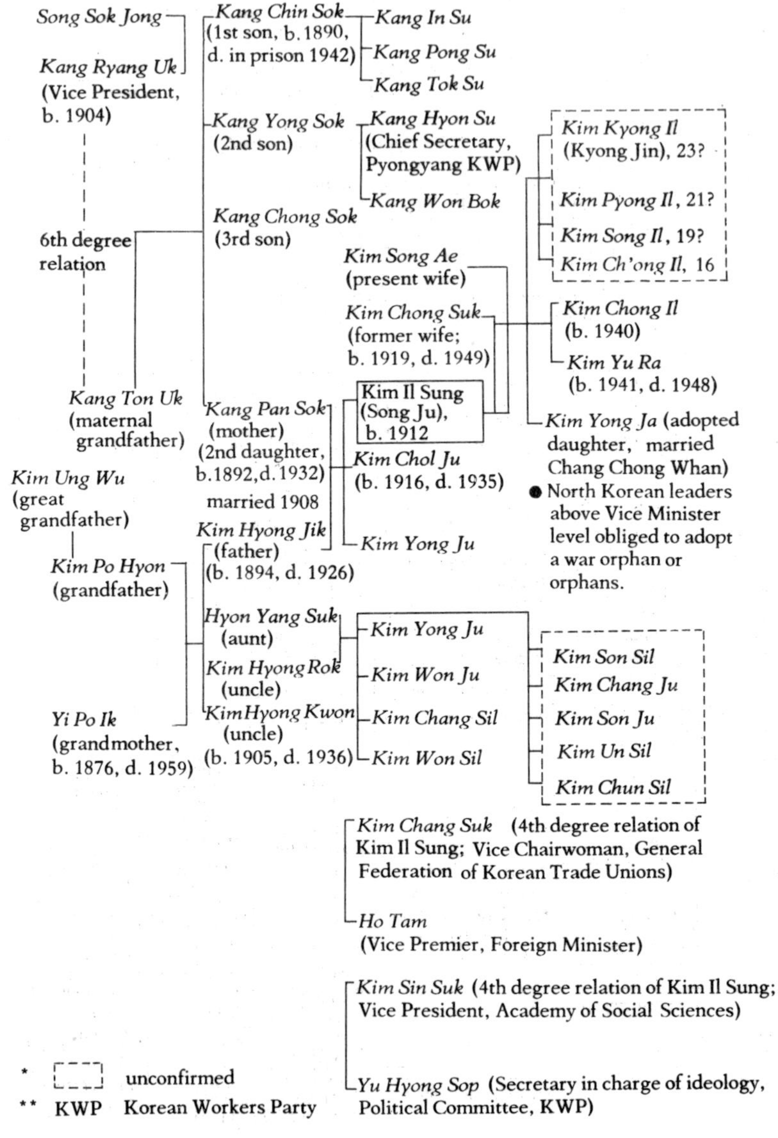

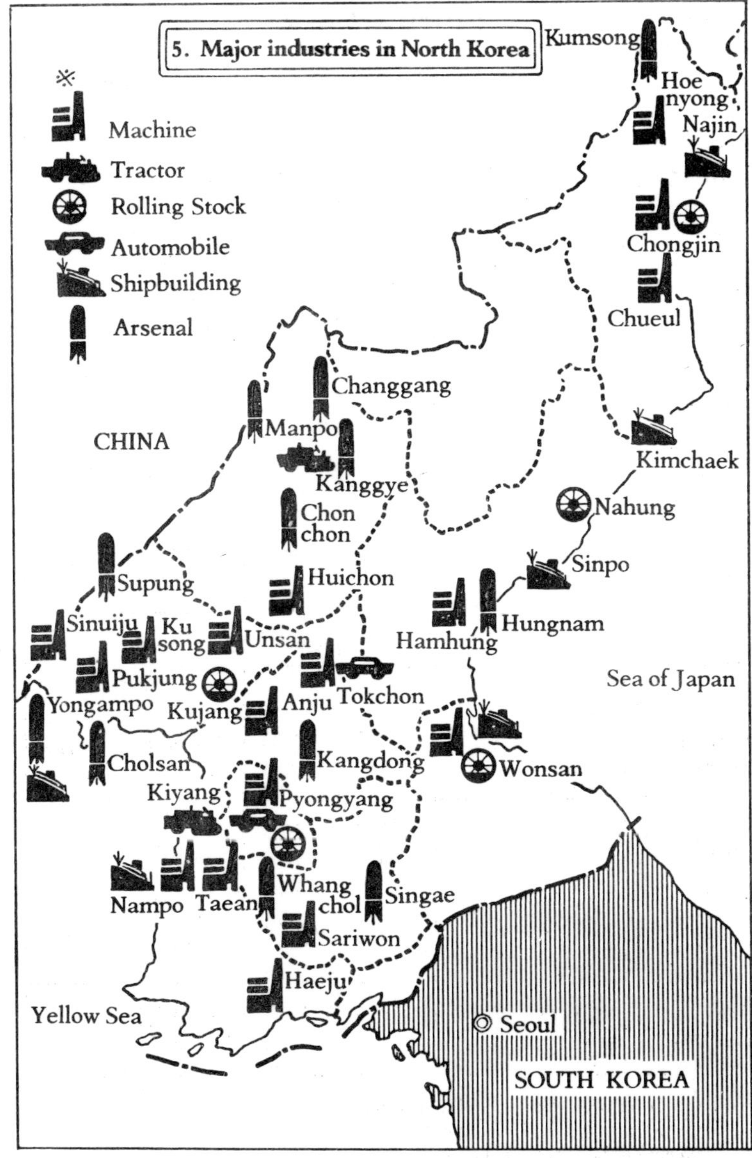

5. Major industries in North Korea
※
Machine
Tractor
Rolling Stock
Automobile
Shipbuilding
Arsenal
CHINA
Kumsong
Hoe nyong
Najin
Chongjin
Chueul
Changgang
Manpo
Kanggye
Chon chon
Kimchaek
Nahung
Huichon
Sinpo
Supung
Hungnam
Sinuiju
Ku song
Unsan
Hamhung
Pukjung
Yongampo
Kujang
Anju
Tokchon
Sea of Japan
Cholsan
Kangdong
Wonsan
Kiyang
Pyongyang
Nampo
Taean
Whang chol
Singae
Sariwon
Haeju
Yellow Sea
Seoul
SOUTH KOREA

6. Economic comparison of the south and the north
—By production of major products —

		Units	1970	1975	1976	South-North ratio as of end of 1976
Electric Power (Production)	S	100 million KWH	91.72	198.37	231.0	1.08
	N	″	165.00	212.98	213.10	
Coal	S	10,000 tons	1,239.4	1,759.5	1,640.1	0.39
	N	″	2,750.0	3,830.0	4,250.0	
Petroleum (refining capacity)	S	″	882	1,514	1,832	18.32
	N	″	—	97	100	
Pig iron	S	″	1.9	118	198.0	0.69
	N	″	202.8	285.7	285.7	
Crude Steel	S	″	48.0	230	344.9	1.00
	N	″	220.0	243.1	344.8	
Automobile	S	Unit	29,147	36,269	49,095	4.09
	N	″	9,000	12,000	— *	
Chemical fertilizer	S	10,000 tons	127.7	181.2	187.8	0.68
	N	″	150	250	275.5	
Cement	S	″	578.2	1,198	1,278	2.05
	N	″	400	575	625	
Textile	S	100 million meters	6.01	15.71	17.43	3.56
	N	″	4.00	4.7	4.9	
Grain (Polished)	S	10,000 tons	694.2	767.2	820.0	1.52
	N	″	347.9	521.0	539.0	

Source: Chong Un Hak, "Nanboku keizaikoryu no kanosei
(A Possibility of South-North Economic Exchange),"
Azia Koron (Seoul), Sept. 1977, p.183.

* The output of 1976 used in working out the South-North ratio.

p. 47   Black – White
        Non-Race – Face

p. 70   English Language Newspapers

p. 163 Importance of Language

p. 175 Freedom

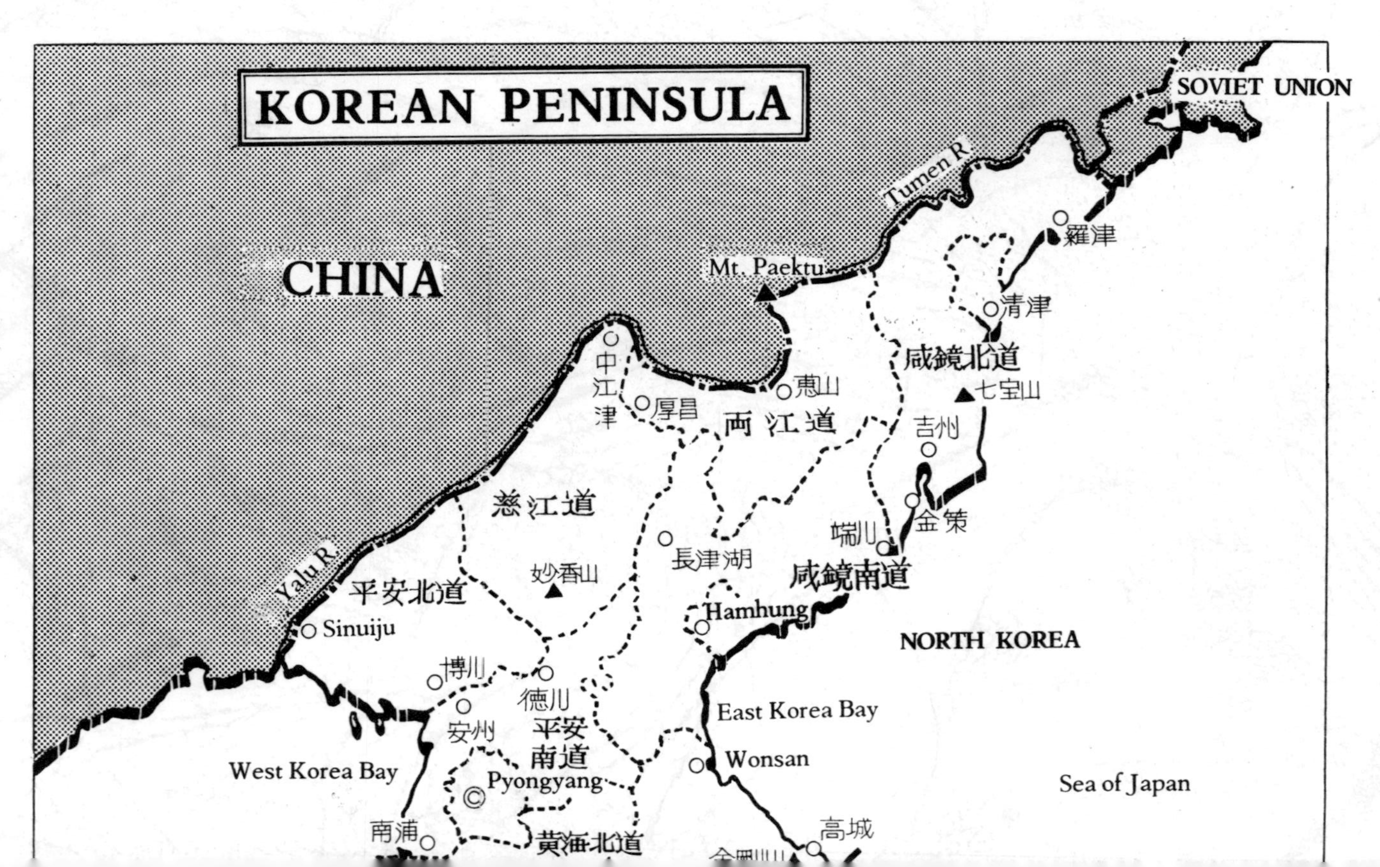

KOREAN PENINSULA
SOVIET UNION
CHINA
NORTH KOREA
Sea of Japan
Tumen R
Yalu R
Mt. Paektu
羅津
清津
咸鏡北道
七宝山
中江津
厚昌
惠山
両江道
吉州
慈江道
端川
金策
長津湖
咸鏡南道
妙香山
平安北道
Hamhung
Sinuiju
博川
德川
安州
平安南道
East Korea Bay
Wonsan
West Korea Bay
Pyongyang
南浦
黄海北道
高城
全羅川山